Challenges and Opportunities for Domest

Josiah Ngula

Challenges and Opportunities for Domestic Tourism in Tanzania

Challenges and Opportunities for Domestic Tourism Development in Tanzania

LAP LAMBERT Academic Publishing

Impressum/Imprint (nur für Deutschland/only for Germany)
Bibliografische Information der Deutschen Nationalbibliothek: Die Deutsche Nationalbibliothek verzeichnet diese Publikation in der Deutschen Nationalbibliografie; detaillierte bibliografische Daten sind im Internet über http://dnb.d-nb.de abrufbar.

Coverbild: www.ingimage.com

Verlag: LAP LAMBERT Academic Publishing GmbH & Co. KG
Heinrich-Böcking-Str. 6-8, 66121 Saarbrücken, Deutschland
Telefon +49 681 3720-310, Telefax +49 681 3720-3109
Email: info@lap-publishing.com

Approved by: Dar es Salaam, University of Dar es Salaam, November, 2010

Herstellung in Deutschland:
Schaltungsdienst Lange o.H.G., Berlin
Books on Demand GmbH, Norderstedt
Reha GmbH, Saarbrücken
Amazon Distribution GmbH, Leipzig
ISBN: 978-3-8484-0832-0

Imprint (only for USA, GB)
Bibliographic information published by the Deutsche Nationalbibliothek: The Deutsche Nationalbibliothek lists this publication in the Deutsche Nationalbibliografie; detailed bibliographic data are available in the Internet at http://dnb.d-nb.de.

Cover image: www.ingimage.com

Publisher: LAP LAMBERT Academic Publishing GmbH & Co. KG
Heinrich-Böcking-Str. 6-8, 66121 Saarbrücken, Germany
Phone +49 681 3720-310, Fax +49 681 3720-3109
Email: info@lap-publishing.com

Printed in the U.S.A.
Printed in the U.K. by (see last page)
ISBN: 978-3-8484-0832-0

ACKNOWLEDGEMENT

I am indebted to many people, individuals and Institutions that in one way or another facilitated the smooth execution of my dissertation. This survey would not have been possible without the dynamic and professional guidance of my supervisor Dr. Diana Philemon a lecturer at University of Dar es Salaam who offered her unwavering support from the time of the research topic Conceptualization to the writing of this report.

I wish to recognize my Marketing research Lecturer Dr. Mwaipopo for sharpening my data analysis and interpretation skills and for his teaching professionalism.

Many thanks to Gloria of TTB information center and Mr Mdamu of MNRT Tourism Division for their support and enthusiasm when addressing my enquiries for information during data collection exercise.

A number of my MBA class colleagues were very supportive during this exercise. I wish to extend my heartfelt gratitude to all of them with special gratitude going to Levina Mfupe and Charles Mung'onya for their kind and unconditional support every time I called upon them.

However I remain entirely responsible for any error, omissions and limitations in this piece of work.

TABLE OF CONTENTS

LIST OF FIGURES   **Page**

LIST OF TABLES   **Page**

LIST OF ABBREVIATIONS

TTB – Tanzania Tourist Board

TD – Tourism Division

WTO – World Tourism Organization

MNRT – Ministry of Natural Resources and Tourism

TANAPA – Tanzania National Parks

UNCED – United Nations Conference on Environment and Development

UN – United Nation

GDP – Gross Domestic Product

BBC – British Broadcasting Corporation

EUROSTAT – Europeans Statistics

EU – European Union

BFEP – Budongo Forest Ecotourism Project

SSS – Sensational Seeking Scale

NAFTA – North American Free Trade Agreement

U.R.T – United Republic of Tanzania

EAC – East Africa Community

UK – United Kingdom

WTTC – World Tourism and Travel Council

IHRA – International Hotel and Restaurant Association

WTTO – World Travel and Tourism Organization

ICLEI – International Council for Local Environment Initiatives

IHEI – International Hotel Environment Initiative

CAST – Caribbean Action for Sustainable Tourism

CHAPTER ONE:
INTRODUCTION

1.0 Background

According to United Nations and World Tourism Organization (UN/WTO), Tourism comprises activities of persons travelling to and staying in places outside their usual environment for not more than one consecutive year for leisure, business and other purposes." The "persons" referred to are termed "visitors", that is "any person, who travels to a place, outside his/her usual environment for a period not exceeding 12 months and whose main purpose of visit is other than the exercise of an activity remunerated from within the place visited". Pigram, (1996:227) defines Tourism as any form of travel that involves an overnight stay.

Leisure activities that do not involve an overnight stay may variously be defined as recreational activities or excursions. The concept of tourism generally involves the act of travel or journeying.

On the other hand domestic tourism refers to any tourism activity within ones country of residence. Burkat and Medlik (1981:82) describe domestic tourism or internal tourism as "the tourist activity of residents of a country within their own country", while Gakuru (1993) defines domestic tourist as a person who travels from his place of residence and goes to another destination within the country and spends her time in enjoying activity or activities which bring him to the destination while paying. The activities could be business, holiday, leisure, visiting friends and relatives or merely moving to another point.

However domestic tourism seems to have escaped the attention of many scholars and practitioners as there is little literature on the subject and even in practice, most people simply talk of tourism which to many simply means visitors from other countries. Some scholars have however managed to come up with some theories on domestic tourism development which have been put into three categories; the development stage theory which suggest that tourism development process goes through a uni-linear change (Archer, 1976). According to Archer, the development of tourism starts with a pioneer resort and there after we have multiplication of resorts which lead to establishment of a hierarchy and functional specialization of resorts. Ultimately the resorts get distributed almost evenly across the country.

Then there is the diffusion theory which argues that at one point of the development process there will be a spread, filtering or simply diffusion of the growth impulses from the most developed region to the less developed one (Young, 1973). The trickledown effect should eventually lead to adjustment to the regional disparities after the initial polarization, and finally we have the dependency theory which is build on the diffusion theory. It maintains that as a result of dependency, capitalism development would continuously create and perpetuate underdevelopment in the periphery (Archer, 1984).

Tourists are expected to travel from their home to another destination. According to Theobald (1994) a tourist is a person travelling for pleasure, for domestic reasons, for health, meeting or in a representative capacity of any kind (scientific, administrative, diplomatic, religious, athletic, etc.) travelling for business. According to the League of Nations (1937), following classes of persons are not regarded as tourists: travelers passing through a country without stopping even if the journey takes more than twenty four hours; students and young persons in boarding establishments or schools; residents in a frontier zone and persons domiciled in one country and working an adjoining country; and persons arriving with or without a contract, to take up occupation or engage in any business activity in the country.

Although 'Tourism' is simply the business of going on holiday it covers a multitude of leisure-time activities ranging from sight-seeing and shopping to attending sports events or visiting friends and relatives. Today film tourism, farm tourism, specialist activities and interest of every kind are extending tourism in new ways and into new regions, while business conferences, trade fairs, study courses and language learning has spread the net even wider (UN/WTO).

Tourism is increasingly growing in importance all over the world where it is making significant contributions to gross domestic product (GDP) in many countries. In some countries tourism is the leading sector, for instance most of the Caribbean islands, the likes of Costa Rica and Bahamas depend mainly on incomes from tourism. Bahamas for instance with a population of only 300,000 people receive an average of 4,000,000 visitors annually. In fact Bahamas has not known anything else other than tourism. In Bahamas tourism is even being taught at primary school level (BBC News program and Macmillan Publishers world statistics). Even Trinidad which is strongly opposed to foreigners and is rich in mineral resources has in the recent years developed this sector because nearly all the neighboring islands have survived mainly on this resource. The leadership has been encouraging development of Micro tourism projects because large scale projects tend to lead to dispossession of land and resources from the local people. They believe that such projects encourage closer interactions between local people and the visitors. In Bolivia, with a population of about 940,000, tourism earn an average of two billion US dollars annually purely from small and medium scale tourism projects (BBC News program and Macmillan Publishers world statistics).

According to Urhausen (2008) in all age cohorts the majority of people make holidays in their country of residence. This finding concurred with Ulrich (2007), who found that most tourists in the European Union are from the EU where 88% of all overnight stays were by either domestic tourist or visitors from other EU-25 member states. 59.1% of the total was by residents while 28.4% were by residents of other EU member states. Only a mere 12.5% were spent by non-resident tourists from countries outside EU.

In United Kingdom (UK) bulk of its tourism is domestic, which has been generating the movement of £67bn around the UK economy, much of it from towns and cities to rural and seaside locations. The "staycation" effect, which has seen many recession-conscious UK residents switch from holidays abroad to holidays at home, is clearly benefiting cultural attractions and, with them, UK tourism. For example, the Tower of London, Hampton Court Palace and Kensington Palace enjoyed their best Easter attendance figures for a decade from domestic tourism. The trend over the last few years has been positive for the British Museum, Edinburgh Castle and Blenheim Palace as well. The National Maritime Museum, which has relied on overseas visitors, has been noticing a sharp spike in attendance from UK residents. Earnings from the 32m people a year who visit from abroad went up to £19bn while Treasury on average gets £15bn a year from domestic tourism *Martin. (2010)*

The two findings exemplifies the important role that domestic tourism play in countries when sufficient facilities to meet the needs and wants of different categories of tourists are well developed across any country or in a region.

1.1 Problem statement

Basically in the developed economies, domestic tourism is well developed. In Israel tourism, is a leading foreign currency earner. While domestic tourism is well developed in Europe in particular, this is not the case in Africa and in Asia. In Africa generally other than Egypt and South Africa, we have limited leisure, recreational and adventure tourism facilities to cater for both domestic and other classes of tourists. Even in Kenya which is one of the leading tourist destinations in Africa, and in which tourism is the second leading foreign exchange earner, these facilities are in isolated and limited in number, whereby domestic tourism is encouraged mainly through subsidized facilities with no comprehensive leisure, recreation or adventure tourist facilities as such.

Likewise in Tanzania, a large proportion of the available facilities are not really worth a visit by a whole family for a day out. The regional integration is set to bring in more customers/visitors to Tanzania which creates a gap between the existing facilities to cater for tourists from the regional market. This gap is to be much wider when we take into account that average Tanzanians are today more able to tour their land due to increased disposable income. Coupled with possible influx of people from the region, expected enhanced economic growth there is a need for extensive domestic tourism facilities development. At the moment we don't seem to have good and attractive facilities that can encourage or befit a tour by ordinary family or people across the country. Available facilities are mainly for upper class and international tourists.

Theme parks across the country plus tourists support services with facilities that meet the needs and wants of ordinary family, Supported by good roads network, quality transport facilities, and affordable accommodation facilities are likely to bridge this gap and to stimulate and encourage domestic tourism. In the words of Swarbrooke, et al "we are living in a time where 'classic' natural wilderness adventure travel is being complemented by adventure experiences in man-made artificial environments, often in urban areas (John Swarbrooke, et. al; adventure tourism, the new frontier)"

In Tanzania there are basically isolated natural tourist attraction facilities, which are too expensive for ordinary Tanzanian because of the explicit and implicit costs of one having to prepare for a separate expedition every time one wishes to take his family or a friend for a weekend outing. More so most of these sites are away from city outskirts making them un-ideal for most of people living and visiting our cities. There is no doubt that we have fantastic national parks, but these are also beyond the reach of the majority of people.

There are good cultural and historical heritages, but these natural attractions alone are not sufficient to cause Tanzanians to travel to other parts of the country. There is a need for diversifying tourist attractions with a focus on those facilities that can be attractive and affordable to domestic tourists rather than over relying on the natural heritages. Why not offer them leisure with recreational and adventure tourism that befits at least a night out for friends or for family members! It is thus time to develop these and other complementary facilities to tap not only domestic tourism but also to create a place worth visiting by international and regional guests. Quality and adequate facilities need to be developed to justify a tour to a given destination or towns.

To encourage people to travel and visit places, we need: Good roads and reliable transport system, good accommodation facilities to cater for different classes of tourists; Good hotels and restaurants, and quality leisure, recreational and adventure tourism facilities such as: Libraries, archives, and museums, incorporating library and museum activities; Museum activities and preservation of historical sites and buildings; Botanical and zoological gardens and nature reserves activities; Sporting activities incorporating: Operation of sports arenas and stadia; Other sporting activities; Recreational activities such as, gambling and betting activities, and other recreational activities not yet classified in different parts of the country that can cater for family, lovers and other types of tourists. (Losekoot and Wood, 'Prospects for Tourism Employment in Scotland,' in Scottish Affairs no. 34, Winter)

If one chooses to go for a holiday in Dar es salaam city or any other city in Tanzania, will it be possible to spend a week in the city, enjoy the stay and come out with a memory of coming back again (the AHA moment)?

The purpose of this study is therefore to investigate the challenges and opportunities for domestic tourism development in Tanzania

1.2 The Objectives of the Study

1.2.1 Main Objective

The general objective of the study was to investigate the challenges and opportunities for domestic tourism in Tanzania

1.2.2 Specific Objectives

To this end the specific objectives of the study was to:

o determine the need and demand level for domestic tourism in Tanzania

o establish extent to which people are satisfied with the current tourism facilities in Tanzania

o identify opportunities and challenges for domestic tourism development in Tanzania

1.3 Significance of the study

In many countries, both developed and developing countries, tourism continues to play important role in the social-economic development. In a number of developing countries tourism remains a major foreign exchange earner and key source of livelihoods especially where the countries are not endowed with mineral resources but endowed with attractive natural heritages and beauty like Tanzania. Many countries have therefore turned into tourism development, for both local and international tourists to capitalize on their natural beauty and heritages. Developed nations have done quite well in domestic tourism development unlike in developing countries where contribution from the sector has been insignificant. Studies have shown that majority of tourists in many countries are from within the country or within a given region. This means there is a need to develop a robust domestic tourism in order to reap full benefits from tourism. It is therefore significant to establish and appreciate the challenges and opportunities associated with domestic tourism which is quite expensive to develop and maintain. Such knowledge would sharpen the understanding of the sector by scholars, policy makers, investors and other stakeholders on issues relating to challenges and opportunities in domestic tourism development and the demand level for Domestic tourism in Tanzania given that there is seldom tangible literature on domestic tourism.

The study has explored many issues relating to domestic tourism sector both globally and within Tanzania, which has exposed the different strategies used to develop and promote domestic tourism, different types of tourist activities, different reasons why people travel world wide, the leisure facilities most preferred by respondents, and global challenges and opportunities in Domestic tourism. This should help stakeholders in the sector when formulating strategies relating to domestic tourism development and promotions.

The domestic tourism theories advanced by (Archer, 1973 and 1984), and (young 1973), have manifested the dynamism in domestic tourism. This should sharpen scholars and encourage stakeholders to appreciate the dynamisms in domestic tourism while providing an opportunity for further studies in the area. The knowledge of diffusion theory for instance should enable policy makers to device policies that can fight back the evils associated with rural urban movement. This is a crucial piece of information as we face the challenges and opportunities for developing domestic tourism in Tanzania.

There exist a huge amount of untapped domestic tourism opportunities in Tanzania, implying that there are potential opportunities for investments in the sector for local and international investors. This should also be seen as a major breakthrough for investment opportunities in the tourism sector in areas such as; infrastructure development and allied services, which is bound to create the needed employment opportunities and enhanced economic growth. However demand for Domestic Tourism is not sufficient in the short run since most of respondents preferred savings and investments to having fun and enjoyment when it came to use of their discretionary income, meaning that the sector should be allowed to grow gradually in the long run. These findings should be useful to the government of Tanzania and private investors in formulating domestic tourism development strategies and in the allocation of their scarce resources and other related decisions.

Since many respondents showed high preference for facilities with affordable accommodation, and facilities that can cater for all categories of tourist imply that theme parks would be ideal area for investments.

CHAPTER TWO:
LITERATURE REVIEW

2.0 Introduction

Literature review involves systematic identification, location and analysis of documents containing information related to the research problem being investigated. It should be extensive and thorough because it is aimed at obtaining detailed knowledge of the topic being studied.

The main purpose of literature review is to determine what has been done already relating to the research problem being studied. A review of the literature will reveal what strategies, procedures and measuring instruments have been found useful in investigating the problem in question. In most cases, literature review will suggest other procedures and approaches.

Another purpose of the literature review is to make the researcher familiar with previous studies and thus facilitate interpretation of the results of the study. In some cases, a researcher may not have narrowed down to atopic at the start of a literature review. In such cases, literature review helps the researcher to limit the research problem and to define it better.

Literature review helps to determine new approaches and stimulate new ideas. Approaches that have proved to be futile will be revealed through literature review. This helps the researcher because there is no point in repeating a certain approach in a study if that approach has been found to be consistently unproductive or unreliable.

Literature review pulls together, integrates and summarizes what is known in an area. A review analyzes and synthesizes different results revealing gaps in information and areas where major questions still remain.

In the case of Domestic tourism, very little literature exists. There was therefore a need to review all relevant materials in order to develop a logical framework for the study.

2.1 Definition of key terms

In this study the following terms will be used to mean as defined below:

2.1.1 Tourism

We will adopt the definition provided by the United Nations and World Tourism Organization, which is more inclusive when compared to other definitions.

Thus tourism comprises the activities of persons travelling to and staying in places outside their usual environment for not more than one consecutive year for leisure, business and other purposes. (WTO, 1994)

2.1.2 Domestic tourism

Domestic tourism or internal tourism is "the tourist activity of residents of a country within their own country" (Burkat and Medlik, 1981:82)

2.1.3 Leisure

Any activity that provide opportunity for enjoyment, self expression, satisfaction and intrinsically motivating (Pigram and Jenkin 1996)

2.1.4 Recreation

Opportunity for enjoyments and self expressions (Pigram and Jenkin (1996)

2.1.5 Adventure tourism

Any activity that provides a tourist with relatively high level of sensory stimulation, whether on artificial environment, natural environment or involving urban exploration (Millington et al, 2001)

2.1.6 Tourist

A tourist is a person travelling for pleasure, for domestic reasons, for health, meeting or in a representative capacity of any kind (scientific, administrative, diplomatic, religious, athletic, etc.) travelling for business (Theobald, 1994)

2.1.7 Excursion

A short outward and return journey, especially for sightseeing or simply on outing (pigram et al, 1996:6)

2.2 Elements of Tourism
2.2.1 Tourism as a Concept

The concept of tourism generally involves the act of travel or journeying. Putting aside any debate over the length of the journey, tourists are expected to travel from their home to another destination. The reliance of tourism on travel is one of the reasons the two are so intertwined. The most convenient 'rule' is that tourism involves an overnight stay. Whilst there is a strong argument for the fact that tourism is undertaken for leisure or recreation purposes, the world tourism organization has taken a slightly broader view of the purposes of tourism. world tourism organization describes tourism: as 'the activities of persons travelling to and staying in places outside their usual environment for not more than one consecutive year for leisure, business and other purposes'(WTO, 1994).

Pigram, (1996: 227), describes tourism as any form of travel that involves an overnight stay. In this case leisure activities that do not involve an overnight stay may variously be defined as recreational activities or excursions.

Although 'tourism' is simply the business of going on holiday it covers a multitude of leisure-time activities ranging from sight-seeing and shopping to attending sports events or visiting friends and relatives. Now film tourism, farm tourism, specialist activities and interest of every kind are extending tourism in new ways and into new regions. Business conferences, trade fairs, study courses and language learning spread the net even wider."

The concept of tourism generally involves the act of travel or journeying. Putting aside any debate over the length of the journey, tourists are expected to travel from their home to another destination. The reliance of tourism on travel is one of the reasons the two are so intertwined. The most convenient 'rule' is that tourism involves an overnight stay. Whilst there is a strong argument for the fact that tourism is undertaken for leisure or recreation purposes, the World Tourism Organization has taken a slightly broader view of the purposes of tourism.

The concept of tourism generally involves the act of travel or journeying. Tourists are expected to travel from their home to another destination. Gakuru (1993) defines domestic tourist as a person who travels from his place of residence and goes to another destination within the country and spends her time in enjoying activity or activities which bring him to the destination while paying. Although 'Tourism' is simply the business of going on holiday it covers a multitude of leisure-time activities ranging from sight-seeing and shopping to attending sports events or visiting friends and relatives. Now film tourism, farm tourism, specialist activities and interest of every kind are extending tourism in new ways and into new regions. Business conferences, trade fairs, study courses and language learning spread the net even wider.

Tourism comprises the activities of persons travelling to and staying in places outside their usual environment for not more than one consecutive year for leisure, business and other purposes." The "persons" referred to are termed "visitors", that is "any person, who travels to a place, outside his/her usual environment for a period not exceeding 12 months and whose main purpose of visit is other than the exercise of an activity remunerated from within the place visited". United Nations and World Tourism Organization: Recommendations on tourism statistics, United Nations, Series M, No. 83, New York 1994, pp. 9, 20, quoted in WTO:

Many definitions of tourism lie within leisure and recreational context, such as Pearce's (1987: 1) conceptualization that 'tourism may be thought of as the relationships and phenomena arising out of journeys and temporary stays of people travelling primarily for leisure or recreation purposes', or Leiper's (1995: 20) suggestion that 'tourism can be defined as the theories and practice of travelling and visiting places for leisure related purposes.

2.2.2 Why people Travel

People are motivated to travel by different reasons: at the outset, a person feels the need to take a break from his or her usual routine. People are intrinsically motivated to enjoy holidays and other forms of leisure for many divergent reasons, including relaxation, prestige, socializing, personal development, desire for something different, excitement, adventure, experiencing different cultures/ways of life, meeting people with similar interests and intellectual enrichment. Crompton (1979); this leads to three different options for the individual: to partake leisure activities within the local area; to take a holiday or travel to see friends and relatives; to travel for business reasons.

2.2.3 Theoretical Explanations of why people Travel

Specific motives shape the nature of the leisure experience, in the form of socio-psychological factors (push factors) and cultural factors (pull factors). Dann (1977); consumer motivation is important in all forms of tourism, including adventure tourism. a number of theoretical frameworks have been devised to explain tourist motivations, but perhaps one of the most applicable to the subject of adventure tourism is the travel career ladder, Pearce, (1988).

The ladder is an adaptation of Maslow's original five-fold hierarchical system of human motivation (Maslow, 1976), and is based on the premise that individuals have a career in their tourist behavior. People seek to satisfy higher level needs or motives through their holidays as a consequence of increased tourism experience. The theory distinguishes intrinsic and extrinsic motivation at the four lower levels of the system, Pearce, (1996: 13).

2.2.4 The travel career Ladder

The travel career ladder emphasizes all the tourists' patterns or motives, rather than a single motive for travelling. The five motivational levels include: a concern with biological needs (including relaxation), safety and security needs (or levels of stimulation), relationship development and extension needs, special interest and self-development needs, and fulfillment of deep involvement needs (formally defined as self actualization).

2.2.5 The Leisure, Recreation and Travel elements of Tourism

Although there are many conceptualizations of leisure, commonly agreed characteristics include the following: it provides opportunities for enjoyment, self expression and satisfaction which makes it intrinsically motivating; it takes place in time set aside from obligation such as employment and family care and is perceived as being freely chosen and entered into by the participant.

Recreation' is often used interchangeably with 'leisure'. Recreation is also voluntarily undertaken, primarily for pleasure and satisfaction, during leisure time but in simple terms the distinction between leisure and recreation is one that identifies leisure with time and recreation with activity. Pigram et al (1999: 6) draw together the ideas of many authors, saying: 'leisure has now become viewed as a process and recreation an experience which is goal oriented, with participation expected to yield satisfactions, and therefore physical and emotional rewards'. Leisure activities that do not involve an overnight stay may variously be defined as recreational activities or excursions.

Hershey, Pennysylvania, the hometown of the chocolate bar, houses not only the company's headquarters but also a 110-acre amusement park. it may not be the gateway parents' dream of, but children seem to enjoy the eight roller coasters, six water rides, more than 20 kiddie rides, monorail, and zoo. At the end of a long day of fun and frolic, families can retire to one of the 235 luxurious rooms in the Hotel Hershey. Source: Hershey foods corporation 1999 annual report; "kids invited," baron's, October 18, 1999, pp.t10-t12.

2.2.6 Types of Tourisms

We have different types of tourism:

2.2.6.1 Nature tourism

Nature tourism involves generally conservation work. it has increasingly been in practice and is contributing to improved living standard of local peoples. For instance in Kenya, Masai people are receiving rent for the lease of their land, plus an entry fee for each tourist visitor to their region. In an inspired piece of reconversion, skilled members of the Masai who had been active in tracking and killing wild animals are now engaged as game scouts and guides and, as wildlife watching has grown, poaching has declined.

2.2.6.2 Ecotourism

Is a concept that describes a form of development that respects tradition and culture, protects and preserves the environment, educates and welcomes visitors, in addition ecotourism should be economically sustainable over the long term. Source: from a 1994 ecotourism business planning guide developed by pacific business centre at the University of Hawaii. A number of ecotourism projects have since been set up and have proved very attractive and useful to tourists and local communities.

For instance in Uganda, the Budongo forest ecotourism project (BFEP) was started in 1993 with the specific intention of involving the local population in forest conservation, the local communities were included in discussions regarding the planning of the project and encouraged to participate in its development and management and by 1997, 28 local people (eight women and 20 men) were employed by the project. The women work as guides, facilitators and caretakers, and the men perform similar tasks, as well as working as trail cutters. Women are able to sell their craftwork at the tourist sites to supplement their income; six primary schools have received assistance through funds provided by the project, while the local community is provided with a forum in which to resolve its conflicts with the forest department.

2.2.6.3 Adventure Travel

This is a leisure activity that takes place in an unusual, exotic, remote or wilderness destination, Millington et al., (2001), it tends to be associated with high levels of activity by the participant, most of it outdoors. These are travelers who are expected to experience various levels of risk, excitement and tranquility, and be personally tested. In particular they are explorers of un-spoilt, exotic parts of the planet and also seek personal challenges. In many text books adventure tourism is seen as a physical phenomenon involving tourists undertaking physical activities in unfamiliar and often inhospitable environments.

Traditionally, adventure tourism meant pitting oneself against nature in an outdoor environment in some way. Consequently though adventure tourists require sleeping accommodation, the nature of it is often very different from that used by mainstream tourists. The most popular forms of accommodation for adventure tourists are: sleeping rough, in the open camping; youth and other hostels; mountain huts and refuges. The transport needs of adventure tourists are of two kinds; first to the destination, and then within the destination. Adventure travelers expect to experience various levels of risk, excitement and tranquility, and be personally tested. In particular they are explorers of un-spoilt, exotic parts of the planet and also seek personal challenges.

2.2.6.4 Non physical adventure Tourism

This can be divided into:

Intellectual adventure, such as travelling for mental self-development;

Emotional adventure, for example gambling or hedonism;

Spiritual adventure, where people travel in search of spiritual enlightenment;

2.2.6.5 Domestic Tourism Adventure

In many countries domestic tourists are the core of the adventure tourism market. People often discover the adventure tourism potential of their country first, and are followed later by foreigners as is the case in New Zealand. Even in a relatively poor country like Botswana, its citizens and residents represented 15 per cent of all visitors to parks and reserves in 1997 (travel and tourism intelligence, 2000). As expected, the USA has a massive domestic adventure tourism market. In 1999, half of USA adults claimed to have taken an adventure trip in the last 5 years. Average expenditure on these vacations was high, at us$1300 per head (travel and tourism intelligence, 2000).

2.2.6.6 Wildlife Tourists

Wildlife tourism is a niche form of ecotourism that encompasses a wide range of products, including safaris, wilderness backpacking, wildlife viewing, aquaria, circuses and zoos, many of which fit under the broad umbrella of adventure tourism. Most wildlife tourism takes place in developing countries, Shackley, (1996). Such countries are exotic destinations and are often renowned for their unique flora and fauna species. Costa Rica, Belize, Antarctica, Namibia, Kenya and Nepal are good examples of world-wide regions that have established wildlife tourism industries. Costa Rica's tourism successes, for instance, are based on its wildlife resources and a well developed system for protecting its natural assets.

2.2.6.7 Rural or nature Tourism

Farmers in traditionally agrarian areas of Europe have had to seek alternative means of supplementing their income by coming up with nature projects that are attractive to other people this partly explains the rise of rural and nature tourism. In the United Kingdom, it is estimated that 90 per cent of all farms provide some form of tourist accommodation. The figures also show that 25 per cent of European holidays are taken in rural, as opposed to coastal areas. The breakup of collective farming in countries in transition to a market economy has also encouraged the spread of rural tourism establishments. Tourists are becoming ever more experienced and are increasingly able to identify their tourism needs and seek out activities that meet them.

2.2.7 Why people seek for Adventure Travels

The sensation seeking scale (SSS); adapted from Zuckerman, (1979) the SSS is a 40-item questionnaire with two choices per item. It comprises an overall measure of sensation-seeking (SSV total), plus four sub-components which explains why people seek for adventure travels:

Thrill and adventure seeking – this category of travelers prefer exciting, adventurous and risky activities (e.g. they prefer remote tourist destinations over well-known ones).

Experience seeking – this category of travelers are characterized by the desire to adopt a non-conforming lifestyle and a tendency to gravitate towards sensations through the senses and mind' (e.g. participating in skydiving to get an 'adrenaline rush').

Boredom susceptibility – this category is looking for a change through avoidance of tedious and unchanging situations. They are characterized by feelings of restlessness when things stay constant for a long time (e.g. going on holiday with the same group of people every year to the same destination and doing the same things). Adventure tourism is 'characterized by its ability to provide the tourist with relatively high levels of sensory stimulation, usually achieved by including physically challenging experiential components with the (typically short) tourist experience. Muller and Cleaver, (2000)

2.2.8 Benefits of adventure travel – travelers (adapted from sung *et al.*, (1997),

Perceived benefits of adventure travel include: discovering new experiences, increased sense of personal growth and educational opportunities.

Activity benefits: fun and excitement, integrated better travel opportunities and outdoor adventure recreation activity participation.

Environmental benefits: improved interpretation of the environment and culture, return to nature, carefree 'Blown away' setting and interaction with environment/people.

Miscellaneous benefits: improved awareness of physical fitness and health, mental and/or physical stimulation other factors not yet known.

2.3 Global Tourism

2.3.1 Changing Tourism Industry

Mass tourism in and from the industrialized countries is a product of the late 60s and early 70s. We are now in "new tourism" era which connotes the idea of responsible, green, soft, alternative and sustainable tourism, and basically refers to the diversification of the tourism industry and its development in targeted, niche markets. Competition in the new tourism is increasingly based on diversification, market segmentation and diagonal integration.

The identification and exploitation of niche markets has proven to be a great source of revenue within new tourism, suggesting that further diversification and customization can be expected in the years to come. Market segmentation – as exemplified by ecotourism, cultural tourism, cruise tourism and adventure tourism – is clearly in evidence and is experiencing great success. New niche markets are constantly being identified in an attempt to diversify the industry further.

2.3.2 Current trends in World Tourism

Scottish tourism has been affected by recent trends in tourism occurring throughout the world. World tourism grew inexorably in the 1990s, with a 52% increase in international trips, and an 80% increase in spending. Growth has been driven by the factors such as: Increased disposable income enabling more people to take holidays and to travel more frequently, increased emphasis on the importance of leisure, health and well-being, the growth of the 'grey market' –people staying active for longer, and being comfortably well off in retirement thus enabling them to take holidays without any strain.

Other factors extend to the desire to have new experiences and to visit new destinations, constantly improving communication and transport systems making the world a 'smaller place', the opening up of previously restricted countries since the fall of communism in eastern Europe has enabled both outbound and inbound tourism for millions of people.

According to Tourism alliance, a lobbying group for the industry, tourism generates £114bn and 2.7million jobs annually. When this is added to all the business involved in hospitality, attractions, events, visitor transport and tourism services, we get to a total of around 200,000 businesses, 80 per cent of which are small and medium-sized enterprises. This demonstrates the potential of tourism to generate employment and to contribute immensely to a nations' economy.

The bulk of UK tourism is domestic which has been generating a movement of about £67billions around the UK economy, much of it from towns and cities to rural and seaside locations. the "staycation" effect, which has seen many recession-conscious UK residents switch from holidays abroad to holidays at home has contributed to this performance while clearly benefiting cultural attractions and hence UK tourism. For example, the Tower of London, Hampton court palace and Kensington palace enjoyed their best Easter attendance figures for a decade. The trend over the last few years has been positive for the British museum, Edinburgh castle and Blenheim palace. The national maritime museum, which has relied on overseas visitors, has been noticing a sharp spike in attendance from UK residents.

Earnings from the 32million visitors a year who visit from abroad amount to the tune of £19billion which is a small amount compared to the 67British pound billions that is earned from domestic tourism. The treasury is on average getting £15bn a year from tourism. *Published date: 25 may 2010; by martin slack*

2.3.3 Promotional strategies
The promotional strategies used in the adventure tourism industry for instance reflect the fact that most players within the sector are small and medium-sized enterprises. In other

words, the emphasis is on finely targeted activities that maximize cost-effectiveness for the typical adventure travel tour operator, the promotional mix could include: the production of a relatively small number of glossy, high-quality brochures, which are not distributed widely but are instead only sent out in response to a specific enquiry.

Website featuring colorful images, factual information, and prices together with a booking facility, there may also be a section containing testimonials from previous customers; exhibits at specialist adventure travel trade shows. Several UK cities now have at least one such show each year, where potential customers visit to look at what is on offer for the following year. one special exhibition in the UK, the adventure travel and sports show, attracted 2000 exhibitors and 28 000 visitors in 2000 (Millington, 2001).

Direct mail marketing particularly to past customers for purpose of encouraging brand loyalty and repeat purchases is another key strategy. incentives may also be offered to existing customers who recommend new potential clients to the organization; obtaining favorable mentions of the company's products in the travel media, including newspapers, magazines and television programs; placing small advertisements in specialist magazines or in the travel supplements of newspapers; doing talks or film shows for potential clients.

2.3.4 Transport & Dispersal of Tourists

To be competitive in the current tourism climate, it has been frequently argued that transportation should be of a good standard. When tourists have a limited time scale, they want to feel that they can get to their intended destination as quickly as possible. Overseas visitors are heavily dependent on the transport system, which has a critical role in spreading the economic benefits of tourism to all parts of the country by making it easy for tourists to travel more widely. Tourist needs for good information services, integrated ticketing, and reliable services and good interchange between networks are no different from those of the resident population. The 2001 British tourism development committee's policy report on *enabling success* argues that "an intuitive, reliable, safe, affordable, and well-marketed transport system is required that takes account of the needs of overseas visitors. The UK's domestic tourism market grew by 49.6% between 1993 and 1997, making it the fastest-growing domestic tourism market among major European countries. Source: Euro monitor publications ltd; ISSN: 0308-3446; year: 1998.

2.3.5 Tourism policy and strategies in Tanzania

The national tourism policy of Tanzania was reviewed in 1999 to cope with the dynamism of the tourism industry. In this review the government considers private investments (both foreign and local) as the engine for growth. To effect implementation of the policy, there is an integrated tourism master plan, which outlines strategies and programs for the sector. The primary focus of this plan is to obtain sustainable benefits for the people of Tanzania by generating additional economic activity from available resources.

The master plan addresses the following areas: creating greater awareness of Tanzania in the tourism source markets; expanding tourism products; securing a more competitive position; maximizing the necessary service skills and; establishing the necessary structures and controls to underpin tourism development. However the national policy does not seem to have given serious consideration for micro domestic tourisms in relation to issues dealing with leisure. For instance there is no mention of plans to tap the domestic tourists through leisure, recreation and or adventure tourism facilities in the Tanzanian tourism marketing strategy. in the national tourism policy of Tanzania reviewed in 1999, there is no mention of leisure, recreation and adventure tourism facilities development for domestic tourism apart from a mention of expanding tourism products, which is not clear the sort of products it wishes to expand.(source: the national tourism policy, sep.199). The government through the ministry of tourism has put a lot of focus and effort on natural attraction areas such as; game parks, historical areas, lakes and mountains.

2.4 Importance of Tourism
Tourism is a major source of foreign exchange earning especially in developing countries which mostly relies on international tourism, it encourages regional integration and creates an opportunity for the spread of a country's soft power.

Tourism encourages community development and improvement in standard of living through development of micro tourism projects such as cultural tourism and ecotourism projects that are common attractions in remote areas leading to increased incomes and hence improved standard of living in remote and less productive areas such the dry and semi arid Maasai land of Kenya and Tanzania, and the semi arid region of Samburu and Turkana in Kenya etc. Tourisms lead to distribution of economic benefits across the nations through small and micro enterprises. It thus provides flexible benefits to local communities over time for different groups.

It is a major catalyst for infrastructural development in remote regions which may lack any other viable economic activity to justify massive investment in infrastructures such as all weather roads, water and power supply. By appealing to a broad cross-section of international and domestic tourists as it does through policies and programs of site and facility development, tourism helps in selling countries' cultural values. It is a major contributor to globalization and integration of global society as it slowly but systematically leads to disintegration of individual cultural values through interaction and sharing of ideas and values.

Tourism help individuals to discover new experiences, increased sense of personal growth and acts as a source of global education by better understanding and interpretation of environment and cultural values. Tourism leads to improved awareness of individual physical fitness and health, mental and physical stimulation especially when we refer to tourism activities involving adventure and recreation, sung et al (1997).

It is a growth sector and continues to be considered as labor intensive with low entry possibilities. Policy makers have therefore tended to view the development of tourism as a way to tackle unemployment and underemployment, especially for persons at the bottom of the labor market, such as the youth, the long term unemployed, the less skilled, ethnic minority groups and women.

2.4.2 Creating Jobs and Wealth

Travel & Tourism is the world's largest industry and creator of jobs across national and regional economies. WTTC research shows that in 2000, travel & tourism will generate directly and indirectly 11.7% of GDP and nearly 200 million jobs in the world-wide economy. These figures are forecasted to total 11.7% and 255 million respectively in 2010. In Tanzania Tourism sector is generating average annual employment of 192,000 as of 2008- Source: The economic survey 2008.

2.4.3 Providing Infrastructure

To a greater degree than most activities, travel & tourism depends on a wide range of infrastructure services - airports, air navigation, roads, railheads and ports, as well as basic infrastructure services required by hotels, restaurants, shops, and recreation facilities (e.g. telecommunications and utilities). It is the combination of tourism and good infrastructure that underpins the economic, environmental and social benefits. It is important to balance any decision to develop an area for tourism against the need to preserve fragile or threatened environments and cultures.

However, once a decision has been taken where an area is appropriate for new tourism development, or that an existing tourist site should be developed further, then good infrastructure will be essential to sustain the quality, economic viability and growth of travel & tourism. Good infrastructure will also be a key factor in the industry's ability to manage visitor flows in ways that do not affect the natural or built heritage, nor counteract against local interests.

2.4.4 Challenge for the Future

Travel & tourism creates jobs and wealth and has tremendous potential to contribute to economically, environmentally and socially sustainable development in both developed countries and emerging nations. It has a comparative advantage in that its start up and running costs can be low compared to many other forms of industry development. It is also often one of the few realistic options for development in many areas. Therefore, there is a strong likelihood that the travel & tourism industry will continue to grow globally over the short to medium term.

2.4.5 Contributing to Sustainable Development

The 1992 UNITED NATIONS conference on environment and development (UNCED), the RIO earth summit identified travel & tourism as one of the key sectors of the economy which could make a positive contribution to achieving sustainable development. The earth summit led to the adoption of agenda 21 a comprehensive program of action adopted by 182 governments to provide a global blueprint for achieving sustainable development. Travel & tourism is the first industry sector to have launched an industry-specific action plan based on agenda 21.

Travel & tourism is able to contribute to development which is economically, ecologically and socially sustainable, because it: it has less impact on natural resources and the environment than most other industries; Is based on enjoyment and appreciation of local culture, built heritage, and natural environment, as such the industry has a direct and powerful motivation to protect these assets. The industry play positive part in increasing consumer commitment to sustainable development principles through its unparalleled consumer distribution channels and provides economic incentives to conserve natural environment and habitat which might otherwise be allocated to more environmentally damaging land uses, thereby, helping to maintain bio-diversity.

2.4.6 Agents and Partnerships for Change and areas for further Action

The challenge facing the tourism industry in moving towards a more sustainable future is set out in "agenda 21 for the travel & tourism industry". To achieve the goals set out in this document require partnership between government departments, national tourism authorities, international and national trade organizations and travel & tourism companies.

Working together in close co-operation such partnerships should be able to deliver: close co-operation between public and private sectors in order to deliver a regulatory regime, which encourages voluntary action while supplementing, where necessary, with regulation in areas such as land-use and waste management, Common standards and tools for measuring progress towards achievement of sustainable development, A more widely applied certification criteria to industry initiatives, Commitment to controlled expansion of infrastructure.

Environmental taxes, where applied, would be non-discriminatory, be more carefully thought out to minimize their negative impact on economic development, and sufficient revenues allocated to travel & tourism associated environment improvement programs.

As a result of the partnership International, national and local funding bodies should include sustainable development as part of their budgetary component, so that in time, all funding would be dependent on sound environmental practice.

Contemporary research into sustainable tourism needs to be funded and developed. Issues requiring attention in this regard include design, carrying capacity, tour operator activities, environmental reporting auditing and environmental impact assessments. Environmental education and training need to be increased, particularly in schools, for future hotel and tourism staff, and greater investment and commitment to the use of new technology. These issues can best be handled through such partnership because of the huge challenges involved which individual stakeholder can not afford.

2.5 Challenges in Tourism Industry

The challenges facing tourism industry globally include: Getting better participation at destination level among all the stakeholders which quite often lead to insufficient collaborations on areas such as land use, plans, outreach programs and tourism ventures; Contradictions and lack of harmonized policies on poverty eradication strategies Ceballos (1996). Lack of cooperation and demand from international tourists who have more money to spend and who may force business people to import goods from far places lead to high prices for local products and food stuff which affects local communities as they cannot afford the prices of foodstuff and other items, honey (1999).

Successful planning for tourism is very important for the future of the industry in coastal regions, because a significant percentage of tourism occurs within the geographical parameters of the definition of a coastal zone. Concerted support from all countries involved (and the industries within them) is vital to protect the shared natural resources that coastal zones represent. Due to vested interests, quite often such collective support does not work out leading to environmental degradation. To circumvent this problem in April 1998, IHEI convened a group of hoteliers, tour operators, architectural firms and sustainable development specialists with the goal of creating a partnership to be called the "sitting and design program". The initiative's mission was to define responsible planning and design specifications that would cause minimal environmental damage at new sites. Particular attention was to be paid to sites located within ecologically sensitive areas and upon waterfronts.

Ensuring linkages with government authorities that uphold responsible development standards would complete the partnership.

Incorporating agenda 21 principles into tourism policies at international and national level, and to promote their inclusion in regional and local strategies is also a major challenge to the industry as a whole.

How governments can help travel & tourism by seeking to minimize regulatory impediments and by offering appropriate investment incentives whereby by supporting tourism and allowing it to compete in open and fair markets, tourism's benefits can be more easily secured. By providing such a lead and establishing a coherent global framework based on agenda 21, national governments can make a vital contribution in developing a more sustainable tourism industry. This remains a major challenge.

2.6 Opportunities in Travel and Tourism Sector

Travel & tourism is a core service sector which should always be considered when looking at policies to expand trade, increase employment, modernize infrastructure and encourage investment - at both domestic and international level. This is because for tourism to thrive, right environment, infrastructure and complementary services are a must leading to massive opportunities.

Developing concerted effort to build up programs for sustainable development is a major opportunity however the sector cannot do it alone. If tourism is to continue to flourish and to contribute to development it has to get help from national governments.

The need for governments to address some of the fundamental barriers to tourism growth by looking at how to expand and modernize infrastructure, to apply taxes fairly and to invest in human resource development creates massive opportunities.

The response to fluctuations in demand, in conjunction with the weight of labor costs, has given rise to strong growth in numerical and functional flexibility in tourism related employment, with relatively high proportions of seasonal and part time workers OECD (1995).

Conserving the natural environment and the development of a comprehensive ecotourism management is yet another opportunity that can be exploited.

2.7 Domestic tourism

2.7.1 Definition

Domestic tourism refers to any tourism activity within ones country of residence. Burkat and Medlik (1981:82) describe domestic tourism or internal tourism as "the tourist activity of residents of a country within their own country", while Gakuru (1993) defines domestic tourist as a person who travels from his place of residence and goes to another destination within the country and spends her time in enjoying activity or activities which bring him to the destination while paying. The activities could be business, holiday, leisure, visiting friends and relatives or merely moving to another point.

World trade Organization (WTO), (1982) describes domestic tourism as activities that involve movement of people outside their normal domicile to other area but within their country of residence. Under domestic tourism, there is free movement of people and no requirements for filling travel documents.

However domestic tourism seems to have escaped the attention of many scholars and practitioners as there is little literature on the subject. Even in practice, most people talk of tourism which to many simply means visitors from other countries.

2.7.4 Importance of domestic Tourism

The following cases exemplifies the importance of domestic tourism as it is in a much better position to address the challenges depicted especially its versatility to niche markets. Source: the British tourism development committee (2001).

Domestic tourism has become a significant market often using the same facilities as international tourists. ST/ESCAP/2478) and it provides opportunities for wealth redistribution and economic development as well as contributing to greater awareness about the culture and environment in one's own country.

2.7.4.1 Changing consumer Preferences

Today, new consumers are influencing the pace and direction of underlying changes in the industry. The "new tourists" are more experienced travelers. Changes in consumer behavior and values provide the fundamental driving force for the new tourism. The increased travel experience, flexibility and independent nature of the new tourists are generating demand for better quality, more value for money and greater flexibility in the travel experience. They reflect demographic changes – the population is ageing, household size is decreasing and households have greater disposable income.

Changing lifestyles of the new tourists are creating demand for more targeted and customized holidays. a number of lifestyle segments – families, single parent households, "empty nesters" (i.e. couples whose children have left home), double income couples without children – will become prevalent in tourism, signaling the advent of a much more differentiated approach to tourism marketing.

Changing values are also generating demand for more environmentally conscious and nature-oriented holidays. Suppliers will therefore have to pay more attention to the way people think, feel and behave than they have done hitherto. In recent years the niche market has become an important factor in the tourism industry reflecting the need to diversify and customize the industry and ensure the sustainability of the product.

The main niche markets (sports travel, spas and health care, adventure and nature tourism, cultural tourism, theme parks, cruise ships, religious travel and others) hold great potential and are developing rapidly. Report for discussion at the tripartite meeting on the human resources development, employment and globalization in the hotel, catering and tourism sector, Geneva, 2001

2.7.4.2 Economic Integration

The world economy is currently witnessing two distinct trends – globalization and regionalization – and within this context states as well as companies are pursuing a variety of different strategies in order to become more competitive. Shifting patterns of production and consumption across the world are also reflected in the rise of new international tourism destinations, particularly in East Asia and in pacific region. This has given rise to increasing regional, intra-regional and interregional competition and to new challenges in terms of investment needs and human resources development, especially with regard to training and labor mobility.

The impact of trade blocs on the hotel, tourism and catering sector can be gauged by the strategies adopted to create an environment conducive to tourism development.

The North American free trade agreement (NAFTA) benefits the travel and tourism industry in many ways. It promotes demand for direct air and charter/tour bus travel in the region, guarantees that tourism companies will receive national treatment in all member countries and maintains high quality of tourism services by encouraging the expansion of telecommunications links between the United States and Mexico.

The 2001 British tourism development committee's policy report on enabling success argues that "an intuitive, reliable, safe, affordable, and well-marketed transport system that takes account of the needs of both local and overseas visitors is required.

2.7.5 Impact of Domestic Tourism at Destination

Figure 1 Impact of Domestic Tourism at Destination

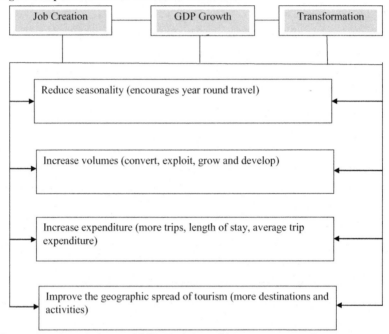

Source: Wineaster Anderson, (2010). Marketing of domestic tourism in Tanzania

This figure essentially summarizes the importance of Domestic tourism and hence the desire to develop and promote this sector. It gives a simplified picture of the positive effects of domestic tourism in a country since for domestic tourism to thrive facilities have to be developed across the country in order to encourage touring the country.

2.7.6 Problems in Domestic Tourism

According to Sustainable development paper presented at RIO Earth Summit 1992 by Brundtland (1987), entitled "Our common future", domestic tourism faces following problems:

First the sector requires immense resources and commitment because most of involves a lot of development of artificial facilities as opposed to natural attraction and more so a lot of infrastructure and complimentary services have to be developed.

It needs stronger political leadership to ensure wide participation and consensus building especially when it comes to resource commitment for development activity.

Raising everyone's interest and support in order to make it sustainable, while it is absolutely necessary, it is pretty difficult due to localized competition and vested individual stakeholders' interests.

2.7.7 An illustrative case for promoting Domestic Tourism

"Tourism experts are today preparing to launch a new drive to attract visitors to don caster, and the town's popular market will be at the centre of the sales pitch. It is hoped don caster will interest tourists from both Britain and abroad; emphasis is being placed on those flying into robinhood airport or arriving on ferries in hull. a new tourism and visitor economy manager has been appointed and a visitor advertisement guide, detailing all the borough's attractions is due to be launched at an event this afternoon. As revealed by the Yorkshire post earlier this year, a group selling don caster "positives" has been set up by the honorary freemen of don caster to combat the criticism. The group, which is independent of politicians or the local authority includes singer Lesley Garrett, who is from Thorne, and Hatfield's TV Sitcom writer Roy Clarke.

Today's event marks don caster council's attempt to join that positive bandwagon, and Mayor Peter Davies said he was backing the new guide and the drive to bring in tourists. He said: "don caster is renowned for its horse racing, with arguably the finest racecourse in the world. It also has a rich railway heritage and wealth of Georgian and regency architecture. It has one of the best markets in the country, it has Cusworth Hall – a grade 1 listed country house and the home of the St Leger – the world's oldest classic horse race. It has one of only three mansion houses in the country, the town is proud of 13 lions at the Yorkshire wildlife park on the edge of the town. And don caster is easy to get to. it is right in the middle of the country with excellent road and rail links, and has the UK's newest international airport with new routes from overseas. The borough is also accessible from the Humber ports. According to council figures, tourism already brings in £285m a year and provides jobs for seven per cent of the local workforce at attractions like the racecourse. Speaking ahead of the events launch, don caster's new tourism manager Colin joy, who spent 19 years working for the national tourist board, said that income could increase. He added: "he was attracted to don caster because there is so much potential for tourism which has been relatively un-tapped so far. Lots of people went to the town either for shopping or for one of the many fantastic events held within the borough, but were unaware of the many attractions within don caster. We are also targeting business people. We want them to come and use our excellent conference and exhibition facilities and also take in some of the sights during their free time here. If we spread the word I'm confident tourists will come. That is the long-term aim, to re-position don caster as a historical market town with a wealth of history, heritage and attractions."

Kurt Jason, policy director of trade association the tourism alliance visited don caster recently and said he supported the town adding: "one thing that really struck me was the quality of the markets. The produce on sale there is at least as good as, if not better than London's famous borough market. The town has an attractive historic heart and a good shopping centre which link up well with the markets. I believe that there is really no reason why don caster should not claim its place on the British tourist trail." this was a press release aimed at marketing don caster as a local domestic destination. I believe that at least every city in Tanzania can be made attractive to domestic tourist, at least every city can have something to be proud of that can be sold to adventure tourists and others. Imagine in UK even something like warm weather is still an aspect for domestic travels as reported in this article. Forecasters predict perfect Staycation conditions as Britain's tourist attractions gear up for a bumper weekend; Matthew weaver guardian.co.uk, Friday 21 may 2010 10.07. Only in the 1990s South America emerged as a potential tourism destination, with Brazil, Argentina and Chile as the main players in the region.

Factors like the transition to democracy, the consolidation of economic blocks, the growth of commerce with the major world markets and the improvement of basic public services, contributed positively to the development of tourism in the region. In conjunction with this the opening up of the markets and massive investments in infrastructure facilitated the flow of tourism to traditional and non-traditional destinations in South America. Gouvea, (2004); Santana, (2000), negative perception about the social and economic conditions in Brazil, as well as the lack of security also creates disadvantage. High cost of domestic transport may influence a country's competitiveness. References: Gouvêa, r. (2004), "managing the ecotourism industry in Latin America: challenges and opportunities", problems and perspectives in management, vol. 2 pp.71-9.

CHAPTER THREE:
METHODOLOGY

3.0 Introduction
3.1 Research design
The subject of the study was a topical problem whose nature was somehow well known and the objectives well specified. It was therefore appropriate to use descriptive research design which took the form of a cross sectional study to provide a snap shot picture of the current scenario of domestic tourism development in Tanzania.

Such a design helped in getting an accurate picture of the nature and the magnitude of challenges and opportunities faced by domestic tourism development in Tanzania. The design was appropriate in the sense that it manifested areas that should be paid attention to by the stakeholders in the tourism industry.

The design managed to capture in details what it takes to develop domestic tourism in Tanzania, captured the challenges and opportunities in domestic tourism development through literature review and discussion with the industries stakeholders.

This is vital information to academic scholars, investors and to the government of Tanzania. It is my hope that the findings would prove to be useful for future decision making as espoused in the research proposal.

3.2 Sample frame
The ultimate goal of this study was to generalize the findings in Tanzania. There was two sample frames. The first sample frame consisted of the population of Dare s salaam region, whose population was projected to be 5,000,000 by end of 2010. The sample frame extended across the three districts of Dar es Salaam region.

The second sample frame consisted of all the stake holders (hotels, concerned ministry, government agencies and tour operators) plus Tanzania tourist board. Due to time limitation six hotel operators were interviewed (two five star hotels; Movenpick and

Kempinisk, two four stars; holiday inn and New Africa; and two star hotels; grand villa and Tamil hotels), three tour operator companies, Tanzania Tourist Board and Ministry of Natural resources and tourism – Tourism division.

3.3 Sample size

The target sample size was 384 units of observations which were to be selected from the three clusters. Over four hundred questionnaires were sent out. Out this number 275 (72%) questionnaires were accepted for further analysis. The expected sample size was arrived at by applying the formulae recommended by fisher et al. The formula is used when there is lack of estimate of proportions as it was the case of the study. Thus 50% is used for p according to fisher;

$n = (z^2 pq)/d^2$

Where

n= the desired sample size when population is greater than 10,000

z= the standard normal deviation at the required confidence level

p= proportion in the target population estimated to have characteristics being measured

q= 1-p; d= the level of statistical significance set.

In our case p=.5, z- statistic = 1.96, at 0.5 confidence level

Thus: $n = [(1.96)^2 2(.05)(.05)]/(.05)^2$

$\qquad = 0.9604/0.0025$

$\qquad = 384.16$

3.4 Units of analysis

The units of analysis comprised of judgment samples of Dar es Salaam region residents, tourism stakeholders and Tanzania tourist board (TTB).

3.5 Types of Data

3.5.1 Secondary Data

Published data was obtained from the ministry of Natural resources and Tourism- tourism division, Tanzania Tourist Board information centre and the three tour operators visited. The hotels did not have useful documented information.

3.5.2 Primary Data

This was obtained through questionnaires divided into two categories; questionnaires administered to residents within Dar es Salaam region. These were simple closed ended questionnaires. In the second category data was collected through the use of open ended questionnaires administered to tourism stakeholders (hotels and tour operators) and Tanzania Tourist Board.

3.6 Sampling Procedure

Clustering sampling technique was used to select the sample studied. Questionnaires were distributed to respondents from the three administrative units (Ilala, Temeke, and Kinondoni) of Dar es Salaam region. Through simple sampling procedure one ward from Ilala and Temeke each, and two wards two wards from Kinondoni were finally selected. Through Judgment sampling techniques, questionnaires were administered to the respondents from the selected wards.

Questionnaires were also administered on the Stakeholders within the selected wards purely on convenient and judgment sampling procedure.

3.7 Data collection Procedures

The data collection involved collecting primary data from residents and the tourism stakeholders; In the case of residents, the questionnaire were handed in to residents of the selected clusters to fill within one week after which they were collected for further analysis. Data from stakeholders were collected by direct interview. Documents containing secondary data were collected at the time of interview but also obtained a number of documents from Tanzania Tourist Board.

3.8 Research Instrument

The research instrument consisted of both highly structured questionnaires and unstructured open ended questionnaires. The closed ended questionnaires were administered to Dar es Salaam residents. This proved to be efficient because it was easy to complete with minimum support. The closed ended questionnaires were of self report itemized rating scales such as: "how happy are you with the way you spend your

47

weekends currently? Please indicate your level of happiness by marking (X) on appropriate box on the scale. These covered three sections: Section one sought to determine respondents' profile and lifestyle in terms of age, education, marital status and gender. Section two sought to determine the need and demand level for domestic tourism in Tanzania. The open ended unstructured questionnaires took the form of a personal interview to the tourism stakeholders and comprised questions such as; what are some of the challenges you have been facing in your attempt to develop your enterprise? This covered section three of the instrument. It aimed at establishing the extend to which people are satisfied with the current tourism facilities in Tanzania and the kind of facilities they would wish to see established in the country.

Second category of the instrument comprised of open ended unstructured questionnaires that was administered directly to tourism stakeholders and sought to identify opportunities and challenges for domestic tourism in Tanzania.

The questionnaire was in English. The sampling method used was judgment sampling method and therefore it was easy to identify those who were willing and able to fill the questionnaire without difficulties and those who willing but needed assistance to complete the questionnaire.

3.9 Data Analysis:
The study was in the form of descriptive survey and as such it involved summarizing data in terms of numbers and frequencies. The data sought were mainly nominal in nature, thus it involved counting without involving any order and checking for any possible relationships and fitness between fairs of different predictor variables was all that could be possibly done. It thus largely involved qualitative analysis whereby according to Olive et al, the data is analyzed systematically in order to make useful conclusions and recommendations. In studies that are largely qualitative in nature, detailed information on the phenomenon being studied is obtained and then attempt is made to establish patterns, trends and relationships. In this study therefore data was analyzed and presented using frequencies, tables of data and charts to facilitate conclusions and recommendations.

Simple descriptive statistics was not going to provide any meaningful information. 450 questionnaires were administered/ distributed to respondents in the four selected clusters. 120 questionnaires from Kinondoni, 80 questionnaires from Temeke and 75 questionnaires from Ilala were accepted for further analysis. To some extent there was gender balance of the respondents with 47.6% female and 52.4 Male and hence the sample was representative enough on the basis of gender.

Majority of the respondents were purposely above 25 years of age, because this is the age group with meaningful income that can be used for touring. Only a few below the age of 25 years are in employment category as most of them are still in schools and colleges. Those above 55 years of age were somehow not cooperative perhaps because they are too busy and have low value to research. Otherwise 77% of the questionnaires accepted for further analysis were received from the age bracket 26-55 years. Only 2.9 was from those above 55years and 17% from those below 26 years.

58% of respondents were married people, 39% were unmarried and 3% were either widows or widowers. This appears to reflect the age distribution, where we had 118 respondents being in the age group 26-35 years. This is where we have large number of those who have just completed their studies, have managed to get their first employment and yet to settle down for a family.

The education distribution was to some extent representative of all levels of education except for primary education where majority categorically refused to take the questionnaires while others demanded payment for them to accept an interview. For those who accepted, requested to do it on their own. Finally of their questionnaires was acceptable for further analysis. Reasons for this negative attitude could be attributed to lack appreciation of the purpose and value of the project. 30% of the respondents were degree holders, 25% diploma holders, 18% postgraduate, 16% high school and 12% secondary level. The diploma holders and degree holders clearly appreciated the work and were approachable too. The postgraduates appreciated the work but were perhaps too busy to find time to complete the questionnaire.

Only 4% of respondents had monthly income below Tshs100,000 per month; 18% had monthly income of more than Tshs700,000 while 78% were in the income brackets Tshs250,000-700,000. This appears to reflect the composition of the respondents in terms of education level and age groups. We had insignificant number of those with primary education and those with postgraduate educations. These are the categories expected to having earnings of less than Tshs100,000 and above Tshs700,000 per month.

67% of the respondents' children are in private schools, and 33% in public schools. This reflects the education level distribution of the respondents where majority were diploma and degree holders. Majority of public schools are taught by less qualified teachers, while private schools have high quality teachers and able to pay better monthly package than public schools, and since diploma and degree holders appreciate quality education, they seem to have opted to take their children to private schools.

Over 60% of the respondents at least owned a car. Only 1.8% owned more than two cars reflecting the small percentage of postgraduate respondents and the number of those with income level above Tshs700,000. This is also in line with the assertion that respondents are still struggling to meet their basic human needs, which could too be the reason why 39.6% of the respondents do not own a car. Thus the high percentage of investment and saving propensity could be on children education, Family residence and to some extent acquiring a car as depicted by data on how the respondents applied their discretionary income where 89% is either saved or invested. Only 11% go enjoying after meeting their necessity of lives. This is also depicted in the small percentage of people with income brackets above Tshs700,000

Cronbach Coefficient Alpha was computed to determine how items correlated among themselves. This is the most commonly used reliability test in social science research. It is a general form of the Kunder-Richardson (KR-20) formula. It provides superior results when compared with other methods of measuring reliability.

3.9.1 Internal Consistency

Table1 Internal consistency test result table

No. of Items used to measure the concept (K)	12
Variance of all scores (S^2)	7.0384
Sum of variances of individual items (s^2)	1.2

CHAPTER FOUR:
FINDINGS AND ANALYSIS

4.0 Introduction

The main objective of the study was to investigate the challenges and opportunities for domestic tourism in Tanzania and specifically to determine the need and demand level for domestic tourism in Tanzania; to establish extent to which people are satisfied with the current tourism facilities in Tanzania and to identify opportunities and challenges for domestic tourism development in Tanzania.

The study was largely qualitative in nature that included some basic quantitative data for clarification purpose and involved collecting data from individual respondents as units of analysis and stakeholders in tourism industry in Tanzania. According to Olive et al, since the study was not empirical nor was it quantitative in nature, there was no need for testing hypothesis nor was there need to apply statistical package. Data were therefore basically analyzed and presented by use of table of frequencies, percentages and charts.

4.1 Findings and Analysis

4.1.1 Response from residences of Dar es Salaam:

Table 2 response from residence

District	No. of respondents
Kinondoni	120
Temeke	80
Ilala	75
Total	275

450 questionnaires were administered/ distributed to respondents in the four clusters selected from the three districts that make Dar es Salaam region. 120 questionnaires from Kinondoni, 80 questionnaires from Temeke and 75 questionnaires from Ilala were accepted for further analysis. The expected number of respondents based on the Fisher

formula for populations above 10,000 was 384. 275 questionnaires were accepted for further analysis as shown above. This represented a response rate of 72% which is statistically a good response.

4.1.1.1 Respondents by Gender

Table 3: Respondents by Gender

Gender	No. of respondents	%
Female	131	47.6
Private school	144	52.4
	275	100

Figure 2

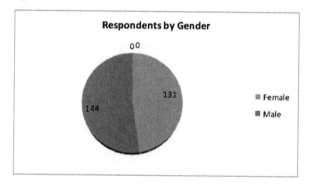

Given that the respondents were selected purely on merit, it means there is near gender balance in Tanzania, with 47.6% of the respondents being Female and 52.4% male. This show that the number of women in gainful employment is rapidly increasing when compared with a few years back when majority of Tanzanian women were mainly house keepers. There is therefore a need to monitor this trend to ensure that right policies and affirmative actions are taken to maintain the gender balance in all sectors of the economy and when coming up with tourism development projects and strategies since these must be pegged on the target customers as well as on market/ customer segmentation.

4.1.1.2 Number of respondents by Age

Table 4: Number of respondents by Age

Age group in years	No. of respondents	%
18-25	49	17.8
26-35	118	42.9
36-45	68	24.7
46-55	32	11.6
56-65	7	2.5
Over 65	1	0.4

Figure 3

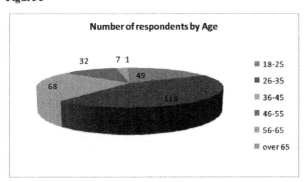

Majority of the respondents were purposely above 25 years of age, because this is the age group with meaningful income that could be used for touring. Only a small number of those below 25 years are is expected to be in employment as most of them are still in schools and colleges. Although a good number of questionnaires were given out to those above 55 years of age somehow they were not cooperative perhaps because they are too busy and have low value to research. Otherwise 77% of the questionnaires accepted for further analysis were received from the age bracket 26-55 years. Only 2.9 came from those above 55years and 17% from those below 26 years.

This is really valuable information, because of other findings such as type of tourism facilities desired by Tanzanians, meaning that if action has to be taken to develop these facilities, the age group that preferred these facilities should be taken into account to ensure that there will be sufficient demand for such projects. The population growth rate and trend should be able to depict how long a project/ facilities are going to remain relevant due to changing age groups. For instance many respondents said they would wish to have facilities with affordable accommodation and those which can cater for all categories of tourists and age groups. Since most of respondents' age ranged between 26 and 45, it implies that such preference is likely to remain viable for foreseeable future.

4.1.1.3 Marital Status of respondents in number

Table 5: Marital status of respondents in number

Marital status	No. of respondents	%
Married	160	58.2
Single	107	38.9
Window/widower	8	2.9

Figure 4

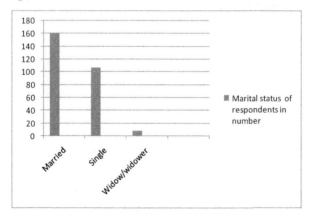

58% of respondents were married people, 39% were unmarried and 3% were either widows or widowers. This appears to reflect the age distribution, where we had 118 respondents being in the age group 26-35 years. This is where we have large number of those who have just completed their studies, have managed to get their first employment and yet to settle down for a family. This could also support the high preference for facilities with affordable accommodation and those which can cater for different types of tourists and age groups, which means facilities that can cater for all family members. The preferences for such facilities should therefore be carefully considered to avoid leaving out other categories of consumers. Otherwise in the not too long future, facilities should cater for the family as a whole.

4.1.1.4 Respondents level of Education

Table 6: Respondents Education level

Education level	No. of respondents	%
Primary	0	0
Secondary	32	11.6
High school	44	16
Diploma	68	24.7
Degree	81	29.5
Post graduate	50	18.2
	275	100

Figure 5

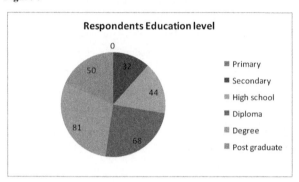

Table 6 shows the sampling was somehow balanced by chance although degree holders were slightly more dominant followed by diploma holders. The results seem to reflect the lifestyle of the respondents as indicated by car ownership as well as the schools attended by the respondents' children.

The education distribution was to some extent representative of all levels of education, although degree holders were slightly more dominant followed by diploma holders. However no questionnaires were returned by respondent with primary education. Many of the respondents expressed initial unwillingness to complete the questionnaire while others categorically refused to take the questionnaires. large size of people with this level of education demanded payment for them to complete the questionnaire. For those who accepted, requested to do it on their own. Finally none of their questionnaires was acceptable for further analysis. Reasons for this negative attitude could be attributed to lack of appreciation of the purpose and value of research project.

Those with higher education appeared to appreciate the importance of the exercise and hence voluntarily completed the questionnaire without much pressure. 30% of the respondents were degree holders, 25% diploma holders, 18% postgraduate, 16% high school and 12% secondary level. The diploma holders and degree holders clearly appreciated the work and were approachable too. The postgraduates appreciated the work but were perhaps too busy with many other issues to find time to complete the questionnaire.

This distribution of respondents closely corresponds to the age, and the type of schools respondents children went to as majority preferred to take their children to private schools because they know the value of good and quality education. Since these are the same respondents who expressed strong desire for facilities with affordable accommodation and those which are able to cater for different types of tourists / different age groups/ family members, it means there is a need to constantly monitor the trend in their demand to ensure that developments of domestic tourism facilities are in line with their demand. However this has to be done in conjunction with other variables such as age group.

4.1.1.5 Type of Schools respondents Children attends

Table 7: Type of Schools respondents' Children attends

Type of school	No. of respondents	%
Public school	77	33
Private school	168	67
	179	100

Figure 6

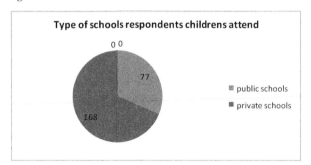

67% of the respondents' children go to private schools which is a clear indication of strong preference for private schools to public one. This corresponds to the respondents' distribution by education where majority of them were either diploma, degree or post graduates. It also supports the strong desire for seeking travels relating to education opportunities. Since they value and understand the importance of education, they have strong preference for quality and good education for their children. Many public schools do not have well qualified teachers and education facilities, while private schools have highly qualified teachers as well as good education facilities.

4.1.1.6 Distribution of Income among the respondents

Table 8: Distribution of net income among the respondents

Income range (in '000)	No. of respondents	%
0000- 0100	11	4
0101- 0250	56	20.4
0251- 0450	73	26.5
0451- 0700	86	31.3
0701- 1000	25	9
1001- 1500	11	4
1501- 3000	13	4.7
Above 3000	0	0
	275	100

Figure 7

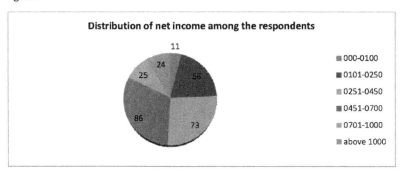

Distribution of net income among the respondents

11
24
25
56
86
73

- 000-0100
- 0101-0250
- 0251-0450
- 0451-0700
- 0701-1000
- above 1000

Table 8 and figure 7 shows the spread of income among the respondents. The most topical income ranged from Tshs 100,000 – 700,000. Majority of the respondents earned between Tshs 451,000 and Tshs 700,000. These are people who completed their diploma or graduated not long time ago and therefore in the early stage of their careers. This is also the group that expressed strong desire for facilities with affordable accommodation because they are energetic and less committed because they are yet to settle down. These are the people with strong preference for adventure tourism.

Only 4% of respondents had monthly income below Tshs100,000 per month; 18% had monthly income of more than Tshs700,000 while 78% were in the income brackets Tshs250,000-700,000. This somehow reflects the composition of the respondents in terms of education level and age groups. We had insignificant number of those with primary education and those with postgraduate educations. These are the categories expected to have earnings of less than Tshs100,000 and above Tshs700,000 per month.

4.1.1.7 Use of Discretionary Income

Table 9: How respondents used their discretionary income

Application	No. of respondents	%
Invest	77	28
Save	168	61
Enjoy themselves	30	11
	275	100

Figure 8

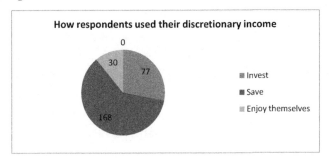

The survey showed that majority of respondents were perhaps busy trying to meet their basic human needs and improving their economic status and living standards as depicted by the high propensity to saving and investment. Only 11% of respondents said they use their disposable income for leisure activities, the rest of respondents said they save or invest their disposable income (balance of income after meeting the necessities of life and taxes). See table 9. This means at the moment massive domestic facilities development is not viable since many people based on this study prefer saving and investments to enjoying themselves. It therefore implies that there is low demand for domestic tourism at the moment. The government should therefore consider putting essential macro-economic measures in place to improve income per capita as well as ensuring even distribution of income in order to stimulate desire for travelling within the country in the long run.

4.1.1.8 Number of cars owned by respondents

Table 10: No. of cars owned by the respondents' family

No. of cars	No. of respondents	%
None	109	39.6
One	109	39.6
Two	52	18.9
More than two	5	1.8
	275	100

Figure 9

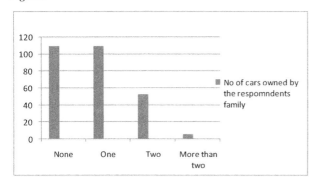

Most of respondents owned at least a car, which to some extent supports their propensity to saving and investment. This can also be associated to difficulties in public transport during rush hours and the fact that many of respondents lived far away from the city business centre where majority work.

Over 60% of the respondents at least owned a car. Only 1.8% owned more than two cars reflecting the small percentage of postgraduate respondents and the number of those with income level above Tshs700,000. This is also in line with the assertion that respondents are still struggling to meet their basic human needs, which could too be the reason why

39.6% of the respondents do not own a car. Thus the high percentage of investment and savings propensity could be on children education, Family residence and to some extent acquiring a car as depicted by data on how the respondents applied their discretionary income where 89% is either saved or invested. Only 11% go enjoying after meeting their necessity of lives. This is also depicted in the small percentage of people with income brackets above Tshs700,000

4.1.1.9 Current satisfaction level of spending weekend

Table 11: Current satisfaction level of spending weekends

Level of happiness	No. of respondents	%
Not happy at all	68	24.7
Not happy	63	22.9
Somehow not happy	48	17.5
Neither	73	26.5
Happy	14	5.1
Happy indeed	3	1.1
Very happy indeed	3	1.1

Figure 10

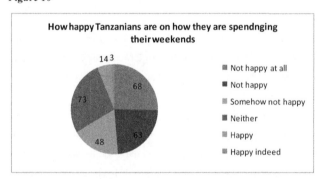

The survey also revealed that most of Dar es Salaam region residents were not happy with the way they are currently spending their weekends/ holidays as depicted by table 11 whereby 65% of the respondents were not happy with the way they are currently spending their weekends, meaning that, they would like to see some changes which is perhaps hampered by family commitments, struggle to meet basic human needs and to upgrade their standard of living as asserted by some stakeholders interviewed. 26.5 % were not sure whether they were happy or not. Only a mere 2.2% seem to be happy about their current way of spending the weekends. This implies that there is a need to improve current tourism facilities and gradually develop additional facilities as well as developing complementary infrastructures to promote domestic tourism.

4.1.1.10 Reasons for going on a Tour.

Table 12: Reasons that would make Respondents go for a Tour

Purpose / reason	No. of respondents	%
To discover new experience	166	60.4
In search of outdoor adventure recreation	125	45.5
To increase sense of personal growth	152	55.3
For educational opportunity	167	60.7
Improved awareness of physical fitness and health	69	25
For fun and excitement	125	45.5
To experience natural environment	90	32.7
For mental and or physical fitness and health	159	57.8
To interact with natural environment	209	76

There was an interesting revelation from respondents on what can make them travel outside their usual place of residence. 76% would move for the purpose of interacting with environment and people. Travelling for education purpose was second in order and was preferred by 60% of the respondents. Interesting enough travelling for fun and excitement, and travelling in search for outdoor adventure recreation which is the view of many people in regard to tourism were placed eighth in the order of preference, implying that the respondents have more important issues to pay attention to other than having fun, excitement and making outdoor adventure recreation. Table 12 summarizes the findings on this. Still the desire for facilities such as nature parks, Eco-tourism, wild life tourism, remote area adventure tourism and other tourism that involve interaction with natural environment are still preferred. Many Tanzanians have acquired their education within the country mostly because of the use of Kiswahili as a media for teaching. Now things have changed and there is increasing use of English in schools, this could therefore be a major motivating factor for the strong preference of travelling for education purpose. This means people are willing and ready to look for quality education whether within or without. Personal growth is also related to desire for education and respondents showed good preference to increase personal growth which could mean intellectual growth and keeping mental and physical fitness which was also highly preferred.

The government should therefore create enabling environment to facilitate development of facilities that can cater for these needs and motives in various parts of the country incase it wishes to stimulate and develop domestic tourism.

4.1.1.11 How Respondents would like to spend their weekends

Table 13: How respondents would like to spend their weekends.

Activity	No. of respondents	%
Stay at home with friends	154	56
Go to have drinks and play pool game	20	7.3
Go out for site seeing	75	27.3
Go out with friends/ family for drinks	139	50.5
Visit leisure joint to have fun	180	65.5

Figure 11

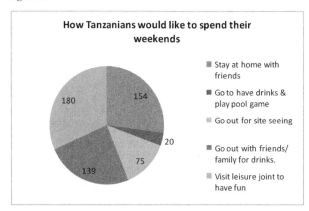

How Tanzanians would like to spend their weekends

- Stay at home with friends
- Go to have drinks & play pool game
- Go out for site seeing
- Go out with friends/ family for drinks.
- Visit leisure joint to have fun

180, 154, 20, 75, 139

65.5% of the respondents would like to spend their weekends in leisure joint with entertainments, while 56% would love to stay at home with friends. This seems to support the findings of how Tanzanians use their discretionary income, whereby 61% of the disposable income is saved. Theme parks with necessary leisure and recreational facilities should be able to cater for the huge desire for fun and outing with friends or family members, while satellite communication facilities, rural and urban electrification programs would facilitate acquisition and use of electronic communication equipments such as TVs, to cater for the 56% of respondents who prefer spending their weekends at home.

4.1.1.12 Leisure Facilities desired by the respondents

Table 14: leisure facilities desired by Tanzanians

Nature of leisure	No. of respondents	%
That thrills (adrenaline activities)	194	70.5
Facility with a lot of fun	145	52.7
With affordable accommodation	202	73.5
With library	95	34.5
With Museum	65	23.6
That caters for different age groups	231	84

Figure 12

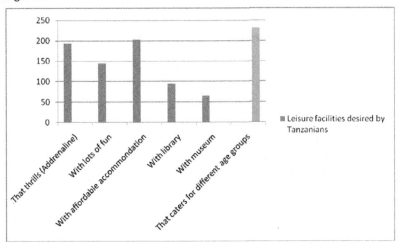

When it came to the kind of facilities that would be attractive (facilities that would stimulate domestic tourism) to the residents of Dar es Salaam region the respondents felt they needed facilities that would offer a combination of leisure activities. Leisure facility catering for people of different age groups or tourists was the most preferred leisure facility, with 84% of the respondents saying they would go for this. 73.5 % of the respondents said they would like to see leisure facilities which offer comfortable accommodation. This was followed by activities that raise adrenaline level which in a way has something to do with fun. 70.5% preferred this. Museum was the least desired facility followed by library services. Perhaps most of respondents have no value for museum, while most of them would prefer to relax in other ways other than reading. Otherwise to many reading is not part of leisure, perhaps there is a need to initiate programs to promote reading culture when we take into account that majority of respondents were high school, diploma and degree holders. This low level preference for library facilities therefore contradicts the expected attributes of the respondents. Concrete research should be carried out to investigate why even highly learned people do not value library facilities/ lacks reading culture.

67

4.2 Secondary Data

4.2.1 Comparative Trends in Earnings from Domestic and International Tourists

Table 15 Tourism trends in Tanzania and foreign currency earnings in millions of US$

Year	Domestic tourism			International Tourism		
	No.	%change	Dollars	No.	%change	Dollars
1990	72,390	-	4.89	153,000	-	65.00
1991	77,732	7.4	6.40	22.09	22.09	94.73
1992	85,880	10.5	18.65	8.00	8.00	120.04
1993	94,902	10.5	10.75	14.09	14.09	146.84
1994	100,485	5.9	53.08	13.65	13.65	192.10
1995	106,207	5.7	49.00	12.89	12.89	259.44
1996	116,135	9.3	44.44	10.46	10.46	322.47
1997	89,892	-22.6	24.64	10.09	10.09	392.39
1998	84,566	-5.9	34.17	34.32	34.32	570.00
1999	82,640	-2.3	12.00	30.00	30.00	733.28
2000	74,990	-9.3	14.89	20.03	20.03	739.06
2001	92,897	23.9	16.40	4.65	4.65	725.00

Source: Ministry of National Resources and Tourism (2002)

The above table gives a summary of earnings received from tourism activity in Tanzania between 1990 and 2001. The earnings are in Millions of US dollars. There is a significant difference between earnings from Domestic tourism and those from international tourists. Unlike in the western countries where domestic tourism leads in earnings, in Tanzania, International tourism earned more than ten times of the domestic earnings in most of the years except the period running from 1994-1996. This in part means that there is still a big gap between the current state of domestic tourism and what it should be, thus demonstrating a market opportunity that should be explored.

There was negative change in domestic earnings from 1997 to 2001, the cause of the negative trend was not explained sufficiently and I think it is important to investigate the cause in order to completely reverse it. During the same period there was increasing earnings trend from International tourism.

The findings in the current survey have shown that the demand for domestic tourism is low as people are busy in trying to meet their basic needs. This to some extent is a reflection of the low earnings from domestic tourism when compared to earnings from international tourism. The government should ultimately develop the sector in the long run, because this is where the real benefit from tourism lies going by what is happening in developed nations.

The government should put strong measures in place to permanently stop the negative growth in earnings from domestic tourism. Possible measures should start with investigating the exact root causes of the poor and declining trend and taking appropriate remedial actions.

To some extent people would find it cumbersome to use foreign currency as a medium of exchange in their own country. This attitude could be a contributing factor to the declining trend in foreign currency earnings from domestic tourism because it means these earnings are mainly from foreigners who are residents in Tanzania but paid in foreign currencies. If this be the case, then why are the earnings systematically declining? An investigation should help to unearth issues that could be vital for the development of the sector.

4.2.2 Domestic and International visitors to the twelve leading parks In Tanzania

Table 16 Domestic and International Visitors to the twelve leading parks in TZ (1987-1998)

| Year | Domestic | | International | |
	No.	%change	No.	Total
1987/88	72,390	-	60,472	132,879
1988/89	77,732	7.4	75,109	152,894
1989/90	85,880	10.5	92,055	177,906
1990/91	94,902	10.5	87,958	186,138
1991/92	100,485	5.9	108967	209,452
1992/93	106,207	5.7	106,272	212,479
1993/94	116,135	9.3	146,392	263,527
1994/95	89,892	-22.6	121,743	237,318
1995//96	84,566	-5.9	175,162	259,905
1996/97	82,640	-2.2	200,830	284,656
1997/98	74,990	-9.3	193,795	269,902

Source: Tanzania National Parks (TANAPA) quick reference statistics.

The twelve leading parks visited are: Serengeti National Park, Lake Manyara National Park, Tarangire National Park, Gombe National Park, Mikumi National Park, Arusha National Park, Ruaha National Park, Kilimanjaro National Park, Katavi National Park, Udzungwa National Park, Mahale National Park, and Rubondo National Park.

The period running from 1987 to 1990 saw domestic tourism leading in number of visits made to the twelve leading parks this trend however changed drastically sharply from 1991 when tours by International visitors more than doubled those of domestic visitors and showing increasing trend, domestic tours assumed decreasing trend.

No sufficient explanation was given for this trend and hence there is a need to investigate the cause for this negative trend for appropriate remedial actions to be taken.

This finding however seem to contradict the findings in the current study, which indicated strong preference for interacting with natural environment. However other desires might have set in to change this preference such as desire for educational travel, desire to discover new experiences and a need to travel for mental and physical fitness purpose.

4.2.3 Visitors to National Museum

Table 17 Visitors to National Museum (1995-2005)

Year	Resident	Non Residents	Total
1995	9,583	4,209	13,792
1996	13,388	6,256	19,644
1997	9,428	4,984	14,412
1998	21,893	8,271	30,164
1999	23,392	6,307	29,699
2000	17,616	5,477	23,093
2001	41,060	12,033	53,093
2002	62,961	15,480	78,441
2003	96,301	13,773	110,074
2004	120,088	11,852	131,940
2005	122,446	13,392	135,838
Total	**538,156**	**102,034**	**640,190**

Source: MNRT (2008). Tourism Statistical Bulletin

Visit to National museum by residents constantly outshone visits by non residents for period running from 1995 to 2001. Perhaps there is a need to improve the standard of museum to make them more attractive to international visitors because the number of visitors is really low even for residents. In fact in this study museum was preferred by only 24% of respondents second to library services from below. This low preference could be based on the past visit experience to museum which were not satisfactory. In Europe, museums are major attractions to both domestic and international tourists. See 2.7.6 – an illustrative case for promoting domestic tourism.

There is a need to modernize our museum facilities, make the inside and outside environment conducive and bearable and improve the quality of artifacts in such museums. And why not! Can't we outsource some of these?

4.2.4 Visitors, Hotel Bed-Nights and Foreign Exchange Earnings

Table 18 No. of Visitors, Hotel Bed-Nights and Foreign Exchange Earnings

Year	2000	2001	2002	2003	2004	2005	2006	2007	2008
Total No. of visitors(000)	502	525	575	576	582	613	644	719	765
Total Bed nights (000)	3837	5549	8430	9600	9625	10,630	11,792	12,748	11,390
Tanzanians	2160	2917	3971	4100	4100	4500	4837	5350	4061
Foreigners	1677	2632	4459	5500	5525	6130	6955	7398	7329

Source: National Bureau of statistics/The economic survey 2008

Domestic tourism world wide contribute more to the economy than International tourism especially in developed countries. However in developing countries there is a tendency for International tourism to bring in more revenue than is from domestic tourism. The table below appears to support this assertion as depicted by higher numbers of Foreigners who stayed in our hotels. Same position is reflected in the 2008 tourists visit to National parks, where again international visitors were far more than local visitors.

For instance the numbers of those who spend nights in Hotels in the year 2000 were 2,160,000 and the trend continued to 2008. This is a small proportion for a country with an estimated population of 40,000,000 people. This shows there is really low demand for domestic tourism and something must be done to promote the sector.

The number of beds occupied by international guests was not either big enough although they were still more than those occupied by Tanzanians, suggesting that there is a need to promote and develop the tourism sector in general.

4.2.5 Number of Tourist Hunters in Tanzania

Table 19 Number of Tourist Hunters in Tanzania

Year	Number of hunter	
	Foreign	Tanzanians
1994/1995	668	194
1995/1996	694	160
1996/1997	937	171
1997/1998	992	355
1998/1999	933	391
1999/2000	923	429
2000/2001	893	407
2001/2002	1035	418
2002/2003	1018	359
2003/2004	1274	380
2004/2005	1245	409
2005/2006	1482	855
2006/2007	1582	855
2007/2008	1508	1725

Source: The economic survey of Tanzania 2008/ wildlife department.

Foreign Tourist hunters are more by over five times to domestic tourist hunters except for the year 2007/2008 where Tanzanians tourists hunters were more than foreigners. This however is an isolated case. The data exemplifies the assertion that domestic tourism in all its meaning is still unexplored, underdeveloped and low. It also supports the field findings of the study whereby many respondents showed low inclination towards spending their income on leisure activities and preference to stay at home or have fun in pubs.

4.2.6 Tourist Visits to National Parks 2008

Table 20 Tourist Visits to National Parks 2008

National Park	Foreigners	Locals	Total	Revenue Generated
Arusha	39,778	43,484	83,262	2,575,599,273
Gombe	1,096	325	1,421	180,902,632
Katavi	3,161	2,250	5,411	231,006,100
Kilimanjaro	155,275	6,954	162,229	28,823,911,461
Kitulo	117	413	530	20,976,100
Ziwa Manyara	11,2687	46,477	159,164	5,081,428,885
Mahale	2,888	191	3,079	480,572,805
Mikumi	21,038	17,629	38,667	776,240, 912
Mkomazi	433	552	985	30,694,500
Ruaha	21,832	12,355	34,187	1,029,601,420
Rubondo	721	490	1,211	64,014,906
Saadani	2482	2,293	4,775	107,269,400
Serengeti	225,606	218,375	443,981	23,266,363, 705
Tarangire	95,760	43,883	139,643	5,075, 470,229
Udzungwa	2,837	1,731	4,563	106,635, 089

Source: TANAPA/ The economic Survey 2008

The trend whereby International tourists are consuming tourism facilities more than the domestic tourists is also reflected in visits to national parks. For instance 155,275 foreigners visited Kilimanjaro national park as compared to 6,954 locals. Likewise huge difference is noted in visit to Tarangire and Serengeti. In total, more foreigners visited the national parks than the locals. When we take into account that locals are charged a highly subsidized rates, it will imply that revenue generated from foreigners who are not only more in number but also charged higher rates is much more.

As stated elsewhere, there is a need to promote and develop tourism among the locals.

4.2.7 Tourist Accommodation in Tanzania

Table 21 Tourist Accommodation in Tanzania (1998-2007)

Description	Unit	2000	2001	2002	2003	2004	2005	2006	2007	2(
Tot. No. of Tourist	No.	501669	525122	575000	576000	582000	613000	644000	719000	7(
No. of tourists in Hotels	No.	479652	501081	550000	522000	553000	590000	605000	673722	7
Total Earnings	US $Ms	739	725	730	731	746	823	950	1037	1
Average earnings per unit	US$	1473	1169	1270	1269	1282	1342	1475	1442	1
No. of Hotels	No.	326	329	465	469	474	495	503	515	5
No. of Hotel rooms	No.	10025	10325	25300	306000	30840	31365	31689	31870	3
No. of Hotel beds	No.	17303	18284	455000	55500	55932	56562	56781	56995	5
Total Tourist bed nights in Hotels	No.	1888000	1955000	8430000	960000	962500	10587000	11792000	12748000	1
Average annual Hotel Occupancy rate	%	54	59	51	47	47	48	48	48	4
No. Employed in the tourist sector	No.	156050	156500	160200	160500	198050	199000	199300	250000	2

Source: MNRT, National bureau of statistics/ The economic survey 2008

On average bed occupation rate is 50%, meaning that there is untapped potential of 50%. This can easily be taken up by domestic tourists. It also implies that tourism in Tanzania is not attractive enough, and therefore a need to do serious promotion of the sector in general. Even the employment generated by the sector is still low when the sector is actually an employment generating engine in many countries. Developing domestic tourism should be able to significantly boost employment creation, spread income distribution and help in transforming rural economy as well as reducing the effect of International tourism seasonality, thus bridging the gap of the huge rate of unoccupied beds.

4.3 Internal consistency of the data

Reliability is the ability to obtain similar results or scores by measuring the same object, trait or construct with independent but comparable measures across time.

Thus:

KR20 = (K) (S^2-Sums^2)/ (S^2) (K-1)

Where:

KR20 = Reliability coefficient of internal consistency

K = Number of items used to measure the concept

S^2= Variance of all scores and

s^2= Variance of individual items

In our case: K= 12; S^2= 7.0384; and Sum of s^2 = 1.2

Thus:

KR20 = 12(7.0384-1.2)/ 7.0384(12-1)

     = 12(6.9184)/77.4224

    = .9049

Cronbach's coefficient Alpha is computed to determine how items correlate among themselves. Its application results in a more conservative estimate of reliability; the estimated coefficient of reliability of data is always lower. To avoid erroneous conclusions, it is always better to underestimate reliability of data than to overestimate. The measure has coefficient ranging from 1 to 0 and a value of 0.6 or less does indicate unsatisfactory internal reliability. A high coefficient implies that items correlate highly among themselves; i.e, there is consistency among the items in measuring the concept of interest. This is sometimes referred to as homogeneity of data. Cronbach's alpha was used because it is the most commonly used reliability test in social science research as it provides the general form of the Kunder- Richardson (K-R)20 formula, and secondly it provides superior results when compared with other methods of measuring reliability. The results of the study had an alpha = 0.9049 while standardized item alpha = 0.8998, this indicates that the data had good internal consistency.

4.4 Challenges in Domestic Tourism Development in Tanzania

4.4.1 General findings

According to Tanzania Tourist Board, challenges facing international tourism development also apply to domestic tourism development because quite often the two categories use more or less the same type of facilities. The country can not have robust domestic tourism unless efficient and essential services such telecommunication services, easy money transfer systems to avoid carrying lots of cash money, internet services, efficient road network as well as good transport system to destination and while at the destination, availability of clean water and energy exist and operational in many parts of the country etc.

According to Ministry of Natural Resources and Tourism – Tourism Division (MNRT-TD); not all tourists come for natural attraction, currently Tanzania is putting her eggs in one basket, there is therefore a need for diversification of the product to include man made facilities such as theme parks. Developing these theme parks and other complementary services require huge amount of money which the country cannot raise in the short run. There is also a need to improve on what is already in existence to make them move with the demands of time.

Developing adequate infrastructure such as good road networks and quality roads in all parts of the country; constructing and servicing airstrips in towns and cities; attracting sufficient foreign investments for leisure, recreation and adventure facilities (see also The 2007 Tanzania Tourism Sector Survey and The 2006 International Visitors' Exit Survey Report recommendations); accessing donors for recreational facilities such as museums and libraries which are like social goods and less profitable, although they could be made part of theme parks; accessing donors/ investors in theme parks, which are generally mammoth projects and hence requiring large capital investment. Inadequate qualified and competent human capital; these would need to be developed through intensive and extensive training both locally and internationally; possibility of other nations duplicating the developments in other parts of the African region;

According to TTB research department getting all stakeholders to work together as an integrated system; creating awareness on the part of those making decisions about tourism development of The social, economic and environmental balance to be pursued in achieving sustainable development; Creating commitment by tourism operators and travelers to contribute to the maintenance of the local environment and culture of the host destination; Strengthening institutional framework with inadequate controls that leads to tourism development which is both appropriate and intrusive; Establishing fairly traded tourism, whereby local communities are able to share in its benefits and ensuring that large flows of visitors in remote or sensitive locations do not place considerable strains on local resources (particularly water) and supply systems is a major challenge.

Travelers' expectations of the goods and services, which should be available, can lead to these items or services, being imported from outside or local supply chains, being distorted to meet demands; and Tourism can change a destination's cultural make-up and, if poorly developed, this can increase crime, prostitution and other social problems especially for poor countries like Tanzania. Although these challenges are more or less common in Africa and in many developing countries' Tanzania should be prepared to take the leadership.

Developing sufficient and competent human resources to coup up with the demands for domestic and international tourist standards is a major challenge in Tanzania due to the attitude of people towards tourism industry. Acts of terrorism which can happen at any moment and at any tourist destination as it happened in Tanzania and Kenya, and recently in Uganda pose major concerns for safety and security! Public health issues such as HIV and AIDS, are also a major concern to Tanzania given that the Current situation is likely to be aggravated by increased tourism activities in the country.

Other specific challenges include:

4.4.2 Promoting Domestic tourism

According to Tanzania tourist board (TTB), promoting domestic tourism is a major challenge particularly in the face of serious lack of sufficient funds to develop desirable facilities because amount allocated in the national budget is hardly enough. They would like to promote it, but then what happens if there is an influx in response to such promotions given that the facilities in existence at the moment can not cater for both international and domestic tourists especially during high season.

4.4.3 Purchasing power

Even where travel charges have been reduced and special rates offered to groups such as university students, secondary schools etc, the rate of travel by residents remained too low to call the short. The operators view is that income is a major contributor to this lack of interest. People have no time and money for higher order needs as they are very busy to meet basic human needs and as such view leisure activities as a waste of money and time. Due to low income people have no time to rest. Many local people view tourism as being too expensive and as a white mans' affair. For instance TANAPA has built affordable accommodation facilities while national parks have really cut their entrance fees to citizens. While an international guest pays $25 as entrance fee to the parks, citizens are allowed in for Tshs 1500.00 but still not many go visiting these places. Presence of international guests lead to higher prices of goods in many tourist destinations these high prices are likely us discourage local people from visiting such destinations. Raising peoples' income to a level that can support sustainable domestic tourism, redistribution of income to increase the number of people with sufficient disposable income, underdevelopment, low standard of living and other competing needs for the limited resources are also critical challenges.

4.4.4 Attitude

To many Tanzanians tourism for a long time was associated with low caliber people, people who had nothing else to do, a sector that attracted people with low morality, children are therefore not encouraged to pursue courses in the hospitality industry and hence churned by many people. The sector is not viewed as a source of gainful employment. This attitude has hampered the development of qualified personnel for the sector. Currently large majority of the well trained personnel in tourism sector in Tanzania are foreigners. It is therefore a major challenge to promote and develop domestic tourism sub sector when there is such a big challenge of locally well trained personnel. However with the establishment of the national college for tourism, shortage of well trained human capital as well as negative attitude towards the sector would be minimized.

4.4.5 Quality accommodation facilities
According to Tanzania tourism sector survey (2009), there is shortage of rooms in prominent tourist attractions. Going by the laws of supply and demand, such a situation lead to higher prices for the rooms which discourage domestic tourism unless the rates are subsidized. However TANAPA has tried to circumvent this though it has not been very successful.

4.4.6 Other challenges
Other challenges include the fact that the Tourism division is in its infant stage, which by itself is a major challenge due to lack of experience and structures, lack of business orientation for many people in the hospitality industry, justification of return from the sector and lack of capital for development etc.

4.5 Opportunities for Domestic Tourism Development in Tanzania
Other than the low preference for applying discretionary to enjoyment, all other variable used in the study revealed existence of numerous opportunities for domestic tourism. There was a strong desire for travelling for education purpose, for personal growth, desire for leisure facilities with affordable accommodation facilities, desire for theme park derived from the strong desire for facilities that can cater for all types of tourists/ age groups/ all family members. All these facilities are generally lacking across the country and therefore offer an opportunity to be developed. However this can only be in the long

run because currently many respondents indicated that they are too busy with struggle to meet their basic human needs first before they can raise their faces towards significant leisure and enjoyment.

Opportunities for domestic tourism in Tanzania according to MNRT-TD and other stakeholders interviewed exist mainly because domestic tourism in the country is essentially unexplored. There is therefore a wide gap between what is expected and what is in place at the moment. To bridge this gap wide range of facilities and services must be put place in the long run to service the improved tourism industry. The economy of Tanzania is growing quite fast. This growth is not only going to leave people with more disposable income but will also create accelerated movement of people from various towns and cities to others within Tanzania as well as movement of people from East Africa member states who may come to Tanzania for things like business and professional services. Such movement would stimulate demand for a wide range of facilities such as quality lodges and hotels, qualified staff, quality service, efficient financial system that will make people move around with less liquid cash, efficient transport and good road network to the destination and within the destination, efficient communication systems including telephone and internet services. Other services and facilities that will automatically be triggered include: pubs, disco halls, guest houses, curio shops, woodcarving, batik shops, tour guide etc.

There is also high demand for hospitality training opportunity to entrench the already acclaimed existing soft power. Change in attitude towards hospitality industry due to global influence and closer interaction among the East Africans would improve the human capital development which is essential for the sub sector.

Global influences and changes working as catalysts for new ways of life; rapid changes in peoples' lifestyles and income levels; re-emergency of enlarged East Africa regional integration is likely to promote utilization of the developed leisure, recreation, and adventure facilities, thus improving their economic viability. Existence of wide range of natural attraction facilities should boost the number of days spend by both domestic and foreign tourists since the range of recreation, leisure and adventure facilities will have increased.

CHAPTER FIVE:
CONCLUSIONS AND RECOMMENDATIONS

This section of the report, the researcher makes conclusion and recommendations based on the study findings. According to Lannon, the conclusion "culminates" the research report. The section is of utmost importance to readers because it answers the question that sparked the collection and analysis of data in the first place. According to Olive et al, conclusion discusses the practical application and implications of the findings. This section pulls the strands together broadly and indicates possible actions. Conclusion leads logically to recommendations. Recommendations on the other hand must be consistent with the purpose of the study, its objectives, the evidence presented by the data and the interpretation given. Recommendations should be practical and achievable.

5.0 Conclusions

Bed occupation rate currently stands at 50% in all hotels in Tanzania on average. This means there is another 50% which remain unutilized and which can easily be taken up by developed domestic tourism. Visit to National parks by citizens as of 2008 had assumed a declining trend as opposed to International tourists which was increasing. 65.5 of all respondents said they would wish to visit leisure joints for fun with 56% saying that they would prefer to stay at home with friends. Only 7.3 % said they consider going for sight seeing, implying low propensity for travelling.

67% of the respondents have their children in private schools, with 79% of them owning at least a car, indicating their most preferred areas of investments. This is supported by the fact that 89% of them use their discretionary income on either savings or investment, with only 11% saying they would prefer to enjoy themselves.

70.5% of the respondents would wish to see leisure facilities with adrenaline activities, while 73.5% would wish to see leisure joints with affordable accommodation meaning current accommodation facilities are out of reach by many. A whole 84% would be glad to see leisure joint that caters for people of all age groups implying that theme parks would be preferable. 78% of all respondents earn between Tsh100,000 and 700,000. This does not look good enough to support robust domestic tourism.

Based on these data from respondents plus discussion held with stakeholders, it can be concluded that there exist opportunities for domestic tourism development in Tanzania since at the moment the sub sector is largely unexplored. However the low level in using discretionary income on leisure activities, desire for staying at home with family as opposed to going out for fun or for adventure travel and practice of taking children to private schools, as depicted by the survey result, implies that the existing opportunities can only be capitalized on in the long run as respondents are still struggling to meet their lower order needs. Thus demand is low for domestic tourism to flourish at the moment.

Further to above conclusion, the survey result and the secondary data from TANAPA, Ministry of Natural resources and Tourism, and the economic survey produced by the ministry of finance and economic affaires suggest that there is low propensity for domestic tourism among Tanzanians which makes it unwise to put a lot of resources towards developing facilities targeting domestic tourism in the short run.

5.1 The main Objectives of the study

The main objective of the study was to investigate the challenges and opportunities for domestic tourism in Tanzania. Facts obtained from discussion with stake holders and the survey carried out within Dare es Salaam region showed that there are huge opportunities for domestic tourism development in Tanzania. The survey depicted strong need and demand for facilities that are capable of meeting the needs of different categories of age groups as well as different types of tourists. The second and third needs and demands were facilities with affordable accommodation and adrenaline activities in that order which means that there are opportunities for developing such facilities across Tanzania as a way of stimulating and encouraging people to tour different parts of the country. Theme parks are therefore the main opportunity for developing Domestic tourism in Tanzania.

On the other hand funds for developing these facilities and their complimentary services were sighted as being the main challenge.

5.2 Specific Objectives

5.2.1   The first specific objective of the study was to determine the need and demand level for domestic tourism in Tanzania.

At the moment, the demand for domestic tourism is low and cannot in the short run justify the huge investment that go with domestic tourism. This is because 89% of respondents preferred to save or invest their discretionary income with only 11% saying that they use it for leisure activities. Likewise in response to the question on how they would wish to spend their weekends, 60% said they would prefer to go to leisure joint to have fun, 56% said they prefer staying at home while 50% would prefer going out with friends or family members for drinks. 27% said they would prefer going out for sight seeing. All these are mere leisure activities and not tourism because a tourist whether domestic or international should involve at least an overnight stay at the destination. However in the long run there will be huge need and demand for domestic tourism since at the moment the sub sector is largely unexplored.

5.2.2   The second specific objective of the study was to establish extend to which people are satisfied with the current tourism facilities in Tanzania

The survey showed that 65.1% of the respondents were unhappy with the current state of leisure facilities. Only 7.3% said they were happy, with 26.5 being indifferent as depicted by table 2. This means there is a need to develop affordable leisure facilities and also to improve what is in existence to meet the needs and wants of the people. Currently existing facilities are out of reach to most people. They are too expensive and not comprehensive enough to offer enough fun, leisure, recreation and relaxation that befit at least an overnight stay. Small scale theme parks in the major towns and cities should be able to cater for this in the short run.

5.2.3   The third specific objective of the study was to identify opportunities and challenges for domestic tourism development in Tanzania.

High preference for travelling for education purpose, the desire to discover new experience, and preference to interact with natural environment were sighted as the main circumstances under which the respondents could be made to move out of their usual place of residence. Creating conducive environment for these activities would therefore provide opportunities for domestic tourism development. The desire for leisure facilities with affordable accommodation (73.5% of respondents preferred this), together with facilities that cater for different age group (84% preferred this), depicts a desire to make an overnight stay by the respondents. Developing affordable facilities and facilities that can cater for people of all age groups to cater for these needs are therefore major opportunities.

From direct interview with stakeholders, huge opportunities have been noted to exist in all aspects of domestic tourism in Tanzania because the sub sector is at the moment unexplored and contributing very little to gross domestic income when compared to what is happening in other countries especially in the developed economies. Specifically opportunities do exist in the transport and communication sector, in the energy and service sectors as well as in accommodation and hotels, camping and camping site facilities etc.

Based on the study the main challenge is the low number of people who are able and ready to spend their discretionary income on leisure. Only 11 % of respondents said they do use their discretionary income for enjoyment. 89% said they save or invest. This is a major challenge given the huge investment requirements for leisure facilities and allied services, while the investors would wish to recoup their investment as soon as possible.

5.3 Recommendations

The purpose of the study was to investigate the challenges and opportunities for domestic tourism development in Tanzania. This would provide policy makers, developers and investors with crucial information for decision making.

5.3.1 Facility development

For domestic tourism to be developed and to thrive, local people must be empowered financially/ economically. Wide range of infrastructural development such as: efficient and good road network in all parts of the country, efficient communication systems, efficient financial system as well as affordable and good accommodation across the country, clean water supply system and energy would make touring the country much more friendly, comfortable and easier. Such infrastructures and facilities are critical and therefore need to be systematically developed in the long run.

People would wish to travel but they also need affordable accommodation, they too need leisure facilities that cater for different age groups. They need facilities with potential for personal growth and experiences. Small scale theme parks in the short run would serve this purpose fairly well.

They need also to enjoy and use modern technology wherever they are, even in the remotest part of the country to communicate with their friends, relatives and government agencies when necessary especially those who may wish to be engaged in adventure tourism. This calls upon energy and communication facilities development.

5.3.2 Training facilities

Concerted effort should be made to develop advanced training facilities in hospitality industry, which is likely to not only create qualified human resource base but also change the entrenched wrong perception of the industry among the people.

5.3.3 Macro- economic measures

In order to travel, income per capita should be good enough to leave people with reasonable disposable income which can then be used for leisure, recreation and adventure activities. Such income should be well distributed among the citizens in order to have more people travelling within the country. To this end necessary macro-economic measures should be put in place to not only improve income per capita but also to ensure that the income is evenly distributed.

5.3.4 People wishes

Based on the view that respondents in the survey expressed unrivalled desire for facilities that can cater for people of all age groups/ different tourist categories, as well as facilities with affordable accommodation and adrenaline activities it is hereby recommended that the government of Tanzania looks into the possibility of developing small scale theme parks in our cities and major towns for the time being. Look at this "Hershey, Pennysylvania, the hometown of the chocolate bar, houses not only the company's headquarters but also a 110-acre amusement park. This park may not be the gateway parent's dream of, but children seem to enjoy the eight roller coasters, six water rides, more than 20 kiddie rides, monorail, and zoo. At the end of a long day of fun and frolic, families can retire to one of the 235 luxurious rooms in the Hotel Hershey. Source: Hershey Foods corporation 1999 annual report. This is a case of the kind of initiatives that can be taken to develop domestic tourism. Theme parks should be able to stimulate desire for travelling among the people which at the moment is not vibrant enough. These facilities should be able to mitigate the low bed occupancy rate and in job creation.

5.3.5 Standing Forum

Lack of concerted effort among the stakeholders was sighted as an impediment. It is therefore recommended that a standing forum for all stakeholders in the sector be formed for developing and reviewing sect oral strategic plan from time to time, setting and monitoring standards to ensure that the stakeholders are integrated into an efficient system. The forum can borrow a leave from The 1992 UNITED NATIONS conference on environment and development (UNCED), the RIO earth summit which identified travel & tourism sector as one of the key sectors of the economy which could make a positive contribution to achieving sustainable development. The earth summit led to the adoption of agenda 21 which is a comprehensive program of action adopted by 182 governments to provide global blueprint for achieving sustainable development. Travel & tourism was the first sector to launch an industry-specific action plan based on agenda 21.

5.5 Limitations of the study and direction for future research

The study was done in Dar es Salaam region only. Future studies may need to consider more regions in the sample with diversity in various variables including incomes which determines the possibility of one touring various attractions.

REFERENCES

Tanzania Travel and Tourism Directory including Pemba and Unguja, 2009 (Published by ZG Design for Tourism Confederation of Tanzania and Tanzania Tourist Board).

The National Tourism Policy, September 1999. By Cooper, C. Fletcher, and J. Gilbert

Shepherd, R. and Wan will, S; (1998) Tourism Principles and Practice. New York: Longman;

Pearce, D (1998) Tourist development. London: Longman;

U.R.T (Sept. 1999) National Tourism Policy. Dar es Salaam; Government Printers;

U.R.T. (2002) Integrated Tourism Master Plan for Tanzania; Strategy and Actions;

WTO Tourism Highlights 2001, Preliminary Edition World Tourism Stalls – Jan. 2002;

EAC (2002) Investment and Development Opportunity in theLake Victoria Basin.

Archer. B; S. Wanhill. 1980. Tourism in Bermuda: An Economic Evaluation. Hamilton:

Bermuda Department of Tourism : Bloom, J. and F. Mostert. 1995. Incentive Guidelines for South African Tourism: Implications and Challenges in the Context of Developing Socio-Political trends.

Tourism Economics 1(1): 17–31: Bodlender, J. A. 1982.

Bodlender, J. A, and T. J. Ward. 1987. An Examination of Tourism Incentives. London: Howarth & Howarth.

Hershey Foods corporation 1999 annual report; "kids invited," Baron's, October 18, 1999, pp.T10-T12.

Leiper, N. (1979). The framework of tourism; Towards a definition of tourism, Tourist and the tourist industry, Annals of tourist research, 6(4), 391-394

Smith, S. (1989). Tourism analysis handbook, London, longman

Okoso-Amaa, K. (1993). Marketization of Tourism; Occasional paper

Chenjah C. (1998). Promotion of Tourism in Tanzania, MBA Thesis, University of Dar es Salaam

Theobald, W. (1994), Global Tourism- the next decade, Butterworth Heinemann, UK

Walker, M. (1993), Domestic Tourism, The unexploited opportunity, Kenya international Tourist Exhibition

Ministry of Natural Resources and Tourism (1999), National Tourism Policy, U.R.T

Ministry of Natural Resources and Tourism (2002), Tourism division, Tourism statistics

Ministry of Natural Resources and Tourism, (2008), Tourism Statistical Bulletin

Young, (1973); Diffusion theory of Domestic development theories

Archer, (1976); Development theory of Domestic development process

Archer, (1984); Dependency theory of Domestic development process

Acott and Asikoglu (2001), A study of Northern Cyprus

John Swarbrooke; Colin Beard, Suzanne Leckie & Gill Pomfret: Adventure Tourism, The new Frontier

Losekoot and wood, prospects for tourism employment in Scotland, in Scottish affairs no. 34 Winter 2001

Santana, G. (2000). " An overview of Contemporary Tourism Development in Brazil", International Journal of Contemporary Hospitality management, Vol.12 No.7, pp. 424-30

The 2007 International Visitors' Exit Survey report, Tanzania Tourism Sector Survey (2009)

Wineaster, Anderson (2010), Marketing of Domestic Tourism in Tanzania

U.R.T The Economic Survey 2008, A annual publication of Ministry of Finance and Economic Affairs.

Olive Mugenda and Abel Mugenda, Research Methods- Quantitative and Qualitative approaches

APPENDIXES

The Questionnaire

Section one

Your name (Optional): [   ]

Age in years: 18-25☐ 26-35☐ 36-45☐   46-55☐ 56-65☐   Over 65 ☐

Marital status: Married☐ Single ☐ Widow/ widower ☐

Gender: Female: ☐   Male: ☐

Highest education level attained:
Primary☐ Secondary ☐ High school☐ Diploma☐ Degree ☐ Post graduate ☐

1. How would you like to spend your weekends?
Stay at home with friends   ☐   Go to have a drink and play pool game   ☐

Go out for site seeing   ☐   Go out with friends/ family for drinks   ☐

Visit leisure joint to   have fun ☐

2. How many cars do your family own?

None ☐   One ☐   Two ☐   Three☐   Four ☐   others ☐

3. How many children do you have? [   ]

4. What school do they go to?   Public ☐   private ☐

5. How much money on average do you spend when you go out on a weekend with family or with your friends in Tshs [   ]

6. How much is your total net income per month in Tshs?

0-100,000☐ 101,000-250,000☐ 251,000-450,000☐ 451,000-700,000 ☐

701,000-1M ☐ 1.001-1,500,000☐ 1,501,000-3,000,000 ☐ above 3M ☐

7. How much money do you spend on average for your necessities of life and taxes per month Tsh [   ]

8. What do you do with the balance of your income after meeting your necessities of life and taxes?   Invest: ☐   Save: ☐   Enjoy myself: ☐

Section two

9. What things make or can make you travel/ tour places outside your usual area of residence within your country? Please mark with an (X) on all that is applicable to you.

To discover new experiences…………………..………… ☐

To increase my sense of personal growth…………… ☐

For educational opportunities…………………………☐

For fun and excitement …………………………………… ☐

To search for outdoor adventure recreation………….. ☐

To experience natural environment (to return to nature) ☐

To interact with environment/ people .... ▢

Improved awareness of physical fitness and health...... ▢

For mental and or physical fitness and health............ ▢

Section three

10. How happy are you with the way you spend your weekends currently? Indicate your level of happiness by marking (X) on one of the boxes.

Not happy at all   Very happy indeed

1	2	3	4	5	6	7

11. I would like to see leisure facilities in our towns and cities:

That thrills: ▭   With lots of fun: ▭   with affordable accommodation: ▭

With library: ▭   With museum: ▭ That caters for different age groups: ▭

Thank you very much.

GUIDING QUESTIONS FOR DOMESTIC TOURISM STAKEHOLDERS

Q1:   What is the bed occupation rate per year in your hotel/ hotel industry?

Q2:   How many beds are occupied by residents of Tanzania and how many are occupied by international tourists.

Q3:   What kind of facilities for recreation, leisure or adventure activities do you have in your hotel/ do we have in the tourism industry in Tanzania?

Q4:   Are these facilities sufficient to offer efficient tourism activities in the country?

Q5:   How satisfied are tourists with the current state of tourist facilities in Tanzania?

Q6:   What kind of facilities do they wish were available in the country/ in your hotel?

Q7:   In your opinion what type of tourist facilities/ infrastructure do you consider essential for developing robust tourism (for both domestic and international tourists) sector

Q8:   Why are the facilities/ infrastructures not well developed in the country/ in your hotel at the moment?

Q9:   What problems are faced by the tourism industry in Tanzania?

Q10:   How easy is it to travel within the country by road, by air, or by other means?

Q11:   What challenges have you been facing in your effort to develop tourism facilities?

Q12:   Are these challenges having toll to all stakeholders?

Q13:   Based on your experience from other parts of the world, are the challenges you are facing unique to Tanzania?

Q14:   In your opinion how developed is domestic tourism in the country?

Q15:   What opportunities are there for developing domestic tourism in the country?

Q16:   Have you been putting some effort to develop domestic tourism?

Q17:   What challenges have you been facing in your effort to develop the sector?

Q18:   How supportive is the government in developing domestic tourism?

Q19:   What contributions has the government made specifically for developing domestic tourism

Q20:   How attractive is tourism sector to foreign and local investors in Tanzania?

Q21:   How are the regulatory conditions for investment in the sector?

Q22:   What impact has tourism development had to the environment?

Printed in Great Britain
by Amazon

83633446R00061